Rich

The Experience Maker

Thanks for coming to the session at Temple Chai!

Here's to remarkable experiences!

PRAISE FOR *THE EXPERIENCE MAKER*

"When it comes to customer experience, you have to 'be amazing or go home.' And that's exactly what Dan Gingiss has accomplished with his new book, *The Experience Maker*. This will become your go-to resource for creating amazing experiences for your customers, and then watching as they tell everyone about it. Dan's professional background, remarkable storytelling ability, and practical advice make this your must-read CX book!"

— **Shep Hyken**, customer service/experience expert and *New York Times* bestselling author of *The Amazement Revolution*

"For every business that suspects their only true differentiator is customer experience, this is the indispensable playbook for making it work."

— **Jay Baer**, founder of Convince & Convert and co-author of *Talk Triggers*

"If an experience happened to you and you never shared it, did it actually happen? The answer is yes. Dan is The Experience Maker. After years of designing experiences, Dan shares with you everything he's learned to help you become an experience maker now and in a post-disruption world."

— **Brian Solis**, world-renowned digital anthropologist, futurist, and bestselling author

"Despite the fact that I'm a sales and marketing guy, I feel it's time we all started talking a LOT more about customer experience. That's why this book by Dan Gingiss is so very important. And what's great about this work is that he has systematized CX, something very few have done well up to this point. So if you're looking for a clear, proven system that will elevate your customer experience, retention, and ultimately sales, this book is a MUST read."

– **Marcus Sheridan**, partner at Marcus Sheridan International/IMPACT
and author of *They Ask, You Answer*

"From in-person interactions to digital conversations, any business that hopes to succeed in the future must combine strategic insights with tactical application to deliver remarkable customer experiences. In *The Experience Maker*, Dan Gingiss brings to bear over twenty years of overseeing customer engagement at Discover, Humana, McDonald's, and dozens of small- and medium-sized businesses. His WISER methodology offers a playbook for creating raving fans in a consistent, scalable fashion that will be valuable to your business regardless of your size, scale, or industry. Stop reading blurbs and just buy this book—you won't be disappointed."

– **Joey Coleman**, speaker, consultant, and *Wall Street Journal*
bestselling author of *Never Lose a Customer Again*

"Remember that one experience that made an impression on you for life? That is this book! Meta, right? Let's face it, if you are a human being, you're in the experience business. Buy this book, make it your bible, and learn how to create big and micro human moments your customers will never forget."

– **Bryan Kramer**, TED Talk speaker and *USA Today*
bestselling author of *Human-to-Human*

"Dan Gingiss crushes it with his new book. *The Experience Maker* is about competing in experience wars not price wars. That is how to build brand loyalty in an economy. This is a great book!"

– **John R. DiJulius III**, chief revolution officer of The DiJulius Group
and author of *The Customer Service Revolution*

"Is your brand's customer experience remarkable? If not (or even if it is), this is your go-to book to up your game! Dan provides a thought-provoking model for you to employ to design and deliver a remarkable experience for your customers. This book is not based on theory; you will find practical and actionable examples that not only bring the concepts to life but also allow you to translate the proprietary model to your business."

– **Annette Franz**, founder/CEO of CX Journey Inc. and author of
*Customer Understanding: Three Ways to Put the "Customer"
in Customer Experience (and at the Heart of Your Business)*

"In *The Experience Maker*, Dan Gingiss delivers a playbook that CMOs have been waiting for to implement industry-leading customer experience marketing. Providing a clear and powerful framework with his WISER model, Dan helps companies in this post-pandemic economy to design the right digital experience to ensure they adapt to changing trends. Strategically focusing on the customer experience in the digital age is no longer an option: Market share will be determined more and more by customer experience. That is what makes *The Experience Maker* all the more timely and important for every CMO *and* CEO to read."

– **Neal Schaffer**, president of PDCA Social
and author of *The Age of Influence*

"A great book on the importance of building a shareable (contagious!) customer experience; another winner from the wise and sparkling pen of Dan Gingiss."

– **Micah Solomon**, customer service turnaround expert
and author of *Ignore Your Customers (and They'll Go Away)*

"Dan Gingiss makes a compelling case for using customer experience as your top marketing strategy. *The Experience Maker* reveals a helpful model and shares numerous examples to help you discover how to get customers talking about your business."

– **Jeff Toister**, author of *The Service Culture Handbook*

"Dan Gingiss has found the secret to building a company that breaks through the competition. In *The Experience Maker*, Dan lays out the blueprint for standing out and succeeding in business today by winning with customer experience. Stop competing and start creating remarkable experiences one customer at a time. This is a book that needs to be shared over and over again. Bravo, Dan Gingiss, for paving the way for the future of customer experience."

– **Jesse Cole**, owner of The Savannah Bananas
and author of *Find Your Yellow Tux*

"2020 changed the customer experience landscape in ways most of us couldn't predict. Dan's WISER approach not only addresses the shifts in the economy and customer behavior, but it also thrives in a world where customer lifetime value is the essential business fortification of every company. This book serves as a perfect blueprint for companies that wish to grow amidst economic calamity."

– **Dennis Wakabayashi**, VP of CX Solutions Delivery at RR Donnelley

"Dan's passion for the power of a memorable customer experience is inspiring, and his ideas for how organizations can routinely deliver it are direct and actionable. In today's hyper-connected world, good news travels as fast as bad news, so every organization has even more incentive to create repeatable processes that make ordinary customer experiences extraordinary. This book will help you lead your organization in building a customer-first growth strategy."

– **Chuck Cohen**, managing director of Benco Dental Company

"Dan approaches customer service like no one else. He puts the heart and purpose into it. I truly believe he was born to teach all the major companies we buy from how to provide an experience leading to customer service on another level. In addition, if you ever experience his style of sharing his custom process via his talks, consulting, and hosting, you will be mesmerized and changed for a lifetime. If you have a team that needs inspiration and process, it needs *The Experience Maker*—hands down!"

– **Marquesa Pettway**, lifestyle business mastermind creator
and Zoom strategist

"Dan Gingiss understands every aspect of customer experience, having worked in corporate environments and advising leaders as a successful entrepreneur. His book provides a wealth of actionable information based on proven best practices. Regardless of skill level, you'll learn a lot and be glad you invested the time to be a better experience maker!"

— **Stacy Sherman**, founder of DoingCXRight®

THE
EXPERIENCE
MAKER

HOW TO CREATE **REMARKABLE EXPERIENCES**
THAT YOUR CUSTOMERS CAN'T WAIT TO SHARE

DAN GINGISS

NEW YORK

LONDON • NASHVILLE • MELBOURNE • VANCOUVER

The Experience Maker

How to Create Remarkable Experiences That Your Customers Can't Wait to Share

Published in New York, New York, by Morgan James Publishing. Morgan James is a trademark of Morgan James, LLC. www.MorganJamesPublishing.com

Morgan James BOGO™

A **FREE** ebook edition is available for you or a friend with the purchase of this print book.

_____

CLEARLY SIGN YOUR NAME ABOVE

Instructions to claim your free ebook edition:
1. Visit MorganJamesBOGO.com
2. Sign your name CLEARLY in the space above
3. Complete the form and submit a photo of this entire page
4. You or your friend can download the ebook to your preferred device

ISBN 9781631954580 paperback
ISBN 9781631954627 eBook
ISBN 9781631954597 hardcover
Library of Congress Control Number: 2020951551

Cover Design by:
Donna Shrader

Interior Design by:
Christopher Kirk
www.GFSstudio.com

Morgan James PUBLISHING Builds

with...

Habitat for Humanity® Peninsula and Greater Williamsburg

Morgan James is a proud partner of Habitat for Humanity Peninsula and Greater Williamsburg. Partners in building since 2006.

Get involved today! Visit
MorganJamesPublishing.com/giving-back

To anyone who has gone out of their way to help a customer, this book is for you.

CONTENTS

Bonus:

TAKE THE 10-DAY CX CHALLENGE!

Y ou're the smart one who bought this book and will soon be inspired to take action at your company. But what about all your coworkers?

First, encourage them to read this book too. It always helps when everyone is "speaking the same language" about customer experience. Consider holding a book club discussion where everyone shares their favorite customer experience story from the book and how it might apply to your business.

Then commit to taking the free **10-Day CX Challenge**! You and your team will be presented with a new customer experience challenge every day for two weeks. These are simple yet effective steps to quickly move your business forward along the customer experience maturity path. The CX Challenge is a complimentary bonus for readers of the book; check it out at **www.10daycxchallenge.com**.

If you need any help along the way, drop me a line at dan@dangingiss.com.

ACKNOWLEDGMENTS

For many years, I have considered winning the J.D. Power Award for Customer Satisfaction at Discover my proudest career achievement. Publishing this book has now moved into that top spot. And like the coveted J.D. Power trophy, it took a village to accomplish the feat.

To my parents: Thank you for your undying support and encouragement, even as you were worried that working for "The Dan" might not be as stable as working for "The Man." And thanks for taking the time to read, edit, and comment on the book manuscript, not to mention listening to my podcast and even sharing your own customer experience stories. I love you both!

To my kids: You have always been so supportive of me, asking great questions about my work, letting me work late when we could be watching TV, giving feedback, and even "liking" my YouTube videos (I won't tell your friends). I am so proud of you both and cherish being your dad.

To my siblings: Your expertise in writing/editing and public relations has been invaluable; it is almost like we have our own in-house agency. Thanks for always being there for me.

To the love of my life: Thank you for loving me unconditionally.

There are so many other people who have either directly or indirectly helped me to publish this book, and I sincerely hope I remember to name them all.

The amazing team at Morgan James Publishing, including David Hancock, Jim Howard, Gayle West, Amber Parrott, Lauren Howard, Taylor Chaffer, and the design team, were so welcoming, supportive, and collaborative. Thanks for making me feel like this project was as important to you as it was to me.

My editor, Angie Kiesling, amazed me by intensely analyzing every sentence and not only making my writing sound better, but also perfecting all the formatting. Any residual errors simply mean I neglected to take her suggestions.

My friend and fellow speaker/author Ann Handley, who graciously agreed to write the foreword to this book, has helped me in ways she probably doesn't even know. From inviting me to speak at her celebrated MarketingProfs B2B Forum event to leaving Yuengling Lager in my hotel room because she knew I couldn't get it at home, to making me laugh out loud with almost every email, Ann has had a big impact on me and my career.

My "Speakerpreneur" coach, Marquesa Pettway, helped me brainstorm and research dozens of branding concepts and led me to finding The Experience Maker™. Her infectious energy, unwavering support, and strategic thinking put my business on a new and exciting path.

My business coach, Bryan Kramer, challenged me to think bigger, shared his expertise and endless marketing resources, supported me every step of the way, and, perhaps most importantly, introduced me to Morgan James Publishing.

The team at Benco Dental, including Chuck, Rick, Terry, Melissa, Lindsay, Rachel, and Eric, provided me with opportunity, support, advice, and friendship throughout the writing and publishing process, and for that I am eternally grateful. A very special thanks goes to Donna Shrader at Benco, who designed the beautiful front cover of this book.

Jordan Howard Whitfield, Katherine Gillham, and the team at Digital Onda did such an amazing job developing my website, creating my first speaker's reel, and designing the "CX light bulb" that appears both in my company logo and on this book's front cover.

Many of the stories shared in this book evolved from the *Experience This!* podcast that I co-host with my friend and fellow speaker/author, Joey Coleman. Whether we are in studio recording an entire season in two days, sharing a stage for a live episode, hosting a game show, or just talking politics, I always think of Joey as a trusted friend and partner.

My profession is filled with amazing thought leaders, and I am honored when my name is mentioned among them. This tight-knit community is always willing to lend a hand, brainstorm an idea, or help a colleague promote a project. Thanks to Jay Baer, Ryan Baker, Jeanne Bliss, Nate Brown, Kate Bradley Chernis, John DiJulius, Mary Drumond, Brian Fanzo, Ryan Foland, Annette Franz, Shep Hyken, Mitch Jackson, Karen McCullough, Scott McKain, Bill Quiseng, Marcus Sheridan, Neal Schaffer, Stacy Sherman, Brian Solis, Micah Solomon, Chris Strub, Jeff Toister, Dennis Wakabayashi, and Jeannie Walters for always being just a phone call (or tweet) away.

Finally, to anyone who has ever attended any of my keynotes, read any of my blog posts, listened to any of my podcasts, watched any of my shows, purchased either of my books, or engaged with me on social media, thank you for allowing me to be part of your life, and thank you for letting me continue to do what I love.

Please visit me at www.dangingiss.com and connect with me on Twitter or LinkedIn to continue the conversation! I'd love to hear *your* story about becoming The Experience Maker at your business.

FOREWORD

"**D**ear Ann: Will you write a 500-600 word foreword to my new book?" —*Dan Gingiss*
  "Dear Dan: Sure." —*Ann*

Hello, friend. I'm Ann Handley.

Dan invited me here to deliver the foreword—literally, the part "before [the rest of the] words."

Plenty of books don't have forewords. So why does this one?

Because a foreword is useful when a book needs a warm introduction and context. And if there is one word that needs a bit of context, it's "experience"—the very subject of this book.

"Experience" is one of those ideas—like "authentic" or "jumbo"—that requires context to be understood. (A shrimp can be jumbo. But so can a jet.)

So what does "experience" mean—in a marketing context? To understand that let's visit Maaemo, a 3-star Michelin restaurant in Oslo, Norway.

I don't even know where to begin to describe what it was like to dine at Maaemo, which, when I visited, was one of the top fifty restaurants in the world.

No menus. No ordering. You just have to roll with it. And what shows up is … well, an adventure:

- porridge with shaved, smoked reindeer heart and brown butter
- fermented trout with spring lettuce
- this postage-stamp-sized thing called a liquid waffle served over mountain tea made from wild herbs found only in Bøverdalen.

- … and fifteen more "experiences" with so much more: like frozen blue cheese. Stinging nettles (stingers neutered). Newborn baby artichokes. Salted sheep bits. And still-quivering oysters and scallops, the latter plump with alcohol and lounging in a hot tub of a briny sauce, like college kids on spring break.

So what's all that have to do with the business of marketing and Dan's book?

Maaemo wasn't memorably remarkable just because of what we ate. (Although the "product" was part of it.)

Nay, nay friends. It was also remarkable for the context, or what happened outside the dining room: its customer journey, its story (and how it told it), and more.

That unforgettable story. Maaemo translates into English as "all that is living." Its close-to-the-earth, raw feel forms the backbone of its story—one that features Chef Esben Holmboe Bang pursuing a herd of mountain sheep through the cold, dark Scandinavian landscape.

A flash of knife, the whites of the animal's eye widened in its final moments. Chef skins the animal right there on a rocky shore, seasons its ribs, and roasts it over a driftwood fire he himself assembled.

Gross? Yeah.

But as much as the story repels some people, it galvanizes others.

It's literally visceral. It's raw. Chef himself is a rebel. He's memorable.

But what's really memorable is the realization that Chef Bang is the real deal, worthy of respect: His kitchen doesn't exactly go to Whole Foods to source those newborn artichokes.

Chef probably pulls them out of the dirt.

With his teeth.

How it creates anticipation. We were to dine at Maaemo on a Wednesday. On Tuesday, Maaemo sent a confirmation email.

We wouldn't be on site for another thirty-six hours. But the staff had already begun prepping for our visit, it said. Your reservation is at 7:30 p.m., it said, but the kitchen would kick into high gear at 8:30 a.m. that day, when it saw what local farmers and vendors dropped at the back door.

That email was an ordinary email you might receive from almost anywhere (a restaurant, a doctor's office, a vendor)—a reminder of any appointment whatsoever.

But Maaemo kicked the ordinary into extraordinary. It worked to powerfully conjure up anticipation in our heads. You couldn't help but wonder … at 12 noon … at 2 … at 3 p.m.: *What showed up at the back door? What are they prepping now?*

"Customer empathy" gets tossed around a lot in marketing. But ultimately it's about not just stepping into your customer's shoes but also walking in them through your own business.

Listen, I could go on. But Dan asked me to write only 500-600 words, and I sense that offstage he's tapping his foot and checking his watch, waiting for me to finish up already.

Which is too bad. I really want to tell you about other things that Maaemo did to extend and enrich the experience.

Like inviting each of the tables in the restaurant one-by-one to ascend a circular center staircase (*Is this the stairway to heaven?*) to visit the glassed-in kitchen and pose for photos. (*It felt like a pilgrimage!*)

And how we shared those photos of us smiling next to that rebel Chef Esben EVERYWHERE! And how Maaemo responded.

But I'm now way more than 600 words in, and Dan is about to cut my mic.

Listen, I know that you aren't a Michelin 3-star restaurant.

You don't have a nursery full of newborn vegetables.

Or a fjord from which to scoop a mackerel for light pickling.

Or a valley full of freelance nettle foragers.

The point worthy of upper-casing every letter is this: **EXPERIENCE IS THE BEST MARKETING.**

I ate this meal four years ago—I still can't stop thinking and writing about it. And that is the power of experience. And that is true whether you sell software, services, solutions … or drunk teenage scallops soaking in a briny tub.

What if we thought more systematically about creating consistently remarkable experiences that matter for our customers?

What if we looked more intentionally at creating extraordinary moments they can't forget?

What if we didn't practice messaging karaoke—singing the same song everyone else sings, mimicking the same words in the same voice—but instead found new and creative and witty approaches that reflect our true identity?

How? *<somewhere offstage I hear Dan clear his throat>*

Friends: Let me introduce you to Dan and the concepts in this book. He'll walk you through all of that:

- *The What* that makes for a remarkable experience.
- *The Why* you need one.
- And most of all—*The How*.

Tuck in now, friends. It's a fun ride.

Ann Handley

Chief Content Officer, MarketingProfs

Author of *Everybody Writes* and *Content Rules*

Publisher of World's Best Newsletter at AnnHandley.com/newsletter

Friend of Dan

P.S. 1018 words. But worth the foreword experience.

INTRODUCTION

My goal with this book is to convince you that a remarkable customer experience can be your best sales and marketing strategy, and then show you how to execute it.

You see, when happy customers share their positive experiences with friends, family, and social media followers, it is far more powerful and persuasive than any brand campaign. But most of the time, companies are so focused on acquiring new customers that they forget to provide positive experiences to their existing customers. That makes things infinitely harder on the sales and marketing teams, which are constantly saddled with higher and higher acquisition goals each year while many existing customers are heading for the competition.

To win with customer experience, companies must first change their outdated mindset.

Let's start with a statement that might be a little bit controversial, especially for people who are in sales: Competing on price is a loser's game.

Just ask the owner of the corner gas station; every time he lowers the price of gas by a penny, the gas station across the street does the same thing. Clearly that's not sustainable, unless the gas stations want to give away the gas for free. Yet competing on price leads to this inevitable conclusion in almost every industry.

Competing on product has also become really difficult, as I'm sure those same gas station owners would attest. After all, they both sell essentially the same products, at the pump and inside their convenience stores.

Consider a company that many cite as one of the most innovative companies in the world: Uber. I talked about Uber in my previous book, *Winning at Social Customer Care: How Top Brands Create Engaging Experiences on Social Media*, noting that it is "such a classic example because it figured out how to create a simple, clean experience for both the customer and the driver."[1] But three years after its launch, Lyft essentially copied Uber.

If one of the most innovative companies in the world can get copied, so can your business.

So if companies can't compete on price and can't compete on product, what's left? The answer is customer experience.

The best part about customer experience is that it's delivered by human beings, and the people at your company are unique. No one else has your human beings, which means that you can provide a customer experience that no one else can.

Throughout this book, I want you to think about two, and possibly three, groups of people:

1. **Your customers.** Think about the experience your customers have in doing business with you. I don't mean their buyer persona, marketing segmentation, or demographic / psychographic profile. Put yourself in their shoes and ask, "What does it feel like to be our customer?" What are the emotions attached to it, and how is the experience different from the competition?

2. **Your employees.** It's long been said that happy employees equal happy customers. We can't expect our employees to provide memorable experiences for our customers if we are not providing them with a great employee experience. Keep employees feeling good about your company, and they'll pass on that feeling to customers.

3. **The customers of your customers.** This group applies to companies that sell to other businesses. After all, the products and services that you sell to your customers likely impact *their* customers directly or indirectly. What is that experience like? If we think about the end-user's experience, which may not be that of our own customers, we can help our customers provide a unique experience for their customers. This ultimately makes their business more profitable, which means they need to buy more from us.

In the following pages, I will present many real-life examples of companies creating remarkable experiences for their customers. Some will be business-to-consumer companies (B2C), and some will be business-to-business (B2B). Some will be within your industry, but it's likely that most will not. Don't be afraid of examples that are outside of your industry or competitive set.

Often companies make the mistake of looking only at their direct competitors for inspiration. Stretch your mind and think about what companies in other industries do and how you can apply that back to your company. After all, your customers are comparing you to every other customer experience they've had.

Each example has a takeaway that you can leverage in your business. Obviously, I really like all the examples, otherwise I wouldn't have included them in the book. However, some of the stories will resonate more with you than others, and that's perfectly fine. The idea is to be inspired by a bunch of them so you can go to work and start sharing ideas about how your business can elevate its own customer experience.

A former boss of mine, who recruited me into my first customer experience role, said he did so because he noticed that I was always wearing the "customer" hat in business meetings. I wanted to make sure that the customer was represented as we were making business decisions, so that revenue and profit were not the only considerations.

When done right, a great customer experience will lead to more revenue and more profit.

I want you to become a customer experience leader in your organization. I want you to be wearing that "customer hat" in every one of your meetings. I want you to be that person who rallies the team to roll up their sleeves and start eliminating customer pain points. I want you to be that person who is always looking to enhance the experience to make it more remarkable.

In other words, I want you to become The Experience Maker™ at your company. And I'm going to show you how.

Ready to get started?

Chapter 1

TRADITIONAL MARKETING IS NO LONGER ENOUGH

So much of marketing today is hit or miss. Imagine an archery target with tons of holes all over the surface along each of the rings. A few hit the bullseye, but most don't. This is often the "going viral" strategy—try a whole bunch of stuff and hope something clicks. Have you ever had an executive come to you and say, "Can't you just make us a viral video?" If only it were that easy.

Businesses are competing against innumerable pieces of content bombarding their prospects and customers every single day. Consider:

- 6 million blog posts are written every day, which equates to about 2.2 billion each year.
- 500 million tweets are sent every day, equating to 182.6 billion each year.
- 2.9 million emails are sent every *second*, equating to 91.5 *trillion* each year.[2]

In other words, it is awfully difficult to stand out with content.

According to HubSpot, 75 percent of people "don't accept advertisements as truth," yet 90 percent "believe brand recommendations from friends."[3]

The answer, then, is not to throw more money at marketing or advertising. That statement comes from someone who spent more than twenty years in Corporate America leading marketing teams at three Fortune 300 companies and two B2B companies.

Let's consider just some of the most popular marketing channels today:

- Email: Almost everyone's inbox is stuffed with emails from friends, family, and brands, so it is difficult to stand out among the sheer quantity of messages. Marketers mistakenly look at email as a "free" channel because often there is no direct incremental cost to sending emails, but getting consumers' attention is becoming harder and harder.

- Television: Other than during the Super Bowl, does anyone watch TV commercials anymore? Digital video recorders (DVRs) allow consumers to bypass commercials with the touch of a button and, not surprisingly, many do.

- Social Media: I often reminded the social media teams I managed at Discover and Humana that absolutely no one wakes up in the morning hoping to hear from their credit card company or health insurer. In social media, the problem is more acute because to gain someone's attention, marketers need to interrupt them from scrolling through their feed of baby pictures and cat videos. Does any consumer want that interruption? Of course not, which is why the companies who use this channel as another "megaphone" to shout their brand message rather than actually engage with customers are losing more customers than they are gaining.

- Search: This is a great channel to invest in because consumers are showing purchase intent with their Google searches. Marketers that commit to becoming the best educators in their industry, as my friend Marcus Sheridan suggests in his outstanding book *They Ask, You Answer*, can quickly differentiate themselves from the competition and win more customers by being a great online resource.

- Direct Mail: Interestingly, this old-school marketing channel still works incredibly well for some industries, including credit card and health insurance companies. Why? Because at least in the United States, we don't receive nearly as much mail as we used to, so we're more likely to read the mail we do get. That said, the term "junk mail" wasn't invented for nothing.

- Telemarketing: Please, just don't. This channel is intrusive, annoying, and generally a horrible customer experience.

💡 Word of Mouth: The "Holy Grail" of marketing, yet the most elusive. It is most easily achieved by creating remarkable customer experiences—literally worthy of conversation.

There is a better way than spending more on marketing, and that is to focus on your existing customers. Listen to your customers, engage with them, and they will become your best marketers. That's right, your existing customers will help you acquire new customers.

So stop constantly saddling your sales teams with unreasonably increasing sales goals every year, and start paying attention to your "leaky bucket."

Almost every business has a leaky bucket. As I previously touched on, most companies are focused on sales growth and bringing in new customers at the expense of the existing customers who are funding the business. Without our existing customers, we're out of business. So why do companies spend so much money and time focused on higher and higher sales and new customer goals yet not nearly as much time with the customers they already have?

Retaining an existing customer is easier and cheaper than acquiring a new one, but the net effect is the same.

My friend Ryan Foland drew one of his famous stick figures for me to illustrate the "leaky bucket" concept. That's clearly me there in the cartoon because as you can see, it's a handsome bald guy. There's that leaky bucket, full of customers that are dropping out of the bottom. But wait! Handsome Bald Guy has a net and is catching these customers before they fall to the ground! Hooray for our hero, Handsome Bald Guy!

You don't have to be bald (or even handsome) to keep your customers from falling. You just have to pay more attention to them and provide them with some remarkable experiences. Do that, and they'll never even think about going to your competitor.

Chapter 2

WHAT PEOPLE SHARE

There's no longer such a thing as an "offline" experience because every experience, no matter where it occurs, can be captured on the smartphone in your pocket and shared with the world in an instant. That should cause companies to ponder whether it would be positive or negative for the brand if an experience were shared with the world. Unfortunately, most brands aren't paying enough attention to consider that.

When we think of the experiences that people share, we often go to negative experiences first. This is due to a psychological phenomenon called the availability heuristic, or "the mental shortcut in which someone estimates whether something is likely to occur based on how readily examples come to mind," according to *Psychology Today*.[4] In social media especially, it's not hard to find complaints about negative experiences.

Sure enough, during keynote speeches, I've noticed a trend: Whenever I ask audience members to raise a hand if they remember the last time they could not wait to tell people about an amazing experience they had with a brand, only a smattering of hands go up. But when I ask the audience to raise a hand if they remember the last time a brand disappointed them, almost everyone in the room raises their hand.

The audience experiment usually results in even higher numbers than a global survey by digital experience platform Acquia, "Closing the CX Gap: Customer Experience Trends Report 2019," where more than 5,000 customers and 500 marketers were surveyed. That study found that 66 percent of consumers could not remember the last time a brand exceeded their expectations, and that in general, nearly half (49 percent) of consumers feel the brands they engage with don't meet their expectations for a good experience.[5]

A study by CX management company Sitel Group, however, found that while nearly a third of customers (30 percent) say that they will share a negative experience on social media or write a negative online review, almost half of consumers (49 percent) say the same thing about a positive experience.[6]

This is a critical conclusion, because it tells us that people are more willing to share positive experiences than negative ones.

Medallia, an experience management platform, and Ipsos, a research and data analytics company, reported similar findings in a separate study.

"Word of mouth is the most common response to a positive experience," the report stated. "When asked what they did when they experienced a positive critical incident, customers report telling their friends and family about it in just under half (47%) of cases . . . a fifth (21%) say they wrote on social media to share the experience or wrote a review on the website/rated the company."[7]

So on average, consumers have trouble remembering positive experiences but are definitely willing to share them when they happen. Negative experiences tend to stick with people longer, and the desire to share those is also very high.

The big problem, then, is that consumers don't have enough positive experiences to share. This is the huge opportunity for companies; if you can be that company that creates positive experiences for your customers, people will share them and you will benefit from free, highly credible marketing.

Companies just haven't given customers enough positive experiences to share yet.

You know what people don't share? It's what my millennial friends call *meh*. No one shares a so-so experience. Can you imagine a friend or colleague telling you about the perfectly average experience they had last night at dinner? Nobody does that; they share at the extremes—positive and negative. Yet the vast majority of experiences we have with companies are *meh*.

Customer experiences affect more than just sharing with friends and family or on social media. They also cause customers to take action.

Medallia and Ipsos asked global customers about the factors that influenced their decisions to choose or continue using particular brands. The top two answers were personal experience (50 percent) and the opinions of friends, family, or known peers (20 percent). Another 9 percent cited other ordinary peoples' opinions online.

Bad experiences often result in the customer taking undesired actions, at least as far as the company is concerned. Sixty-four percent of global consumers claimed to have avoided a brand because of a bad experience they had within the last year, according to Medallia and Ipsos.

Worse, they take others with them.

"Word-of-mouth about negative customer experiences can really deter consumers," the study reported. "Almost half (47%) say they have avoided a brand because they heard or read about someone else's bad experience with it."[8]

Positive experiences, in contrast, lead to highly desirable actions.

According to Medallia and Ipsos, "77 percent of consumers have chosen a product or service from a company or brand because of good experiences they have had with it, and this is consistent across generations. Fifty-nine percent also claim to have made a purchase from a company because they heard or read about someone else's good experiences."[9]

I once had the opportunity to ask Chef Stephanie Izard (of *Iron Chef* and *Top Chef* fame) how she would allocate food quality versus customer experience in terms of importance to success. Although she is a successful restaurant owner, I expected the chef in her to prevail. Instead, she surprised me by saying that the two factors were "50/50."[10] Think about that for a minute: An "Iron Chef" says that the food is only half the battle in terms of winning over diners. Customer experience is equally important.

Izard's interpretation gelled with that of restaurateur Scott Wise, owner of more than a dozen Scotty's Brewhouse restaurants in the Midwest, who told me on a podcast that he is "in the business of customer service."[11] He added that if a restaurant has delicious food but terrible service, it fails because it has no customers. But if a restaurant has great food—or even just good food—and outstanding, memorable service, its customers will remain loyal for years to come.

If companies can shift the *meh* experiences to positive, sharing will increase both on social media and "IRL" (in real life). Our customers will begin marketing our brand for us and in a way that is far more credible than yet another brand marketing campaign. After all, it's always better when someone else says something nice about you versus you telling everyone yourself. More positive experience sharing results is more positive sentiment toward a brand, especially in social media.

Interestingly, some of the most positive experiences come after a customer service interaction, which, almost by definition, means something about the experience wasn't right in the first place.

"In these instances, the goal is to resolve the customer's concerns quickly, effectively, and empathetically," said Tom Karinshak, executive vice president (EVP) and chief customer experience officer of Comcast. "When customer service is done right, we get [the service] back up and running while making sure they feel valued and heard. And when you have a great experience with a company like that, you're going to tell people about it."[12]

As we used to say when I led global social media at McDonald's, the goal is to make the brand lovers louder than the brand haters. It's nearly impossible to get rid of the haters altogether, but it's entirely possible to drown them out in positivity.

Some industries are seeing more positivity than negativity. According to "The Best Brands and Industries for Customer Experience 2020" by digital consumer intelligence platform Brandwatch, the hotel industry leads the way with about 70 percent positivity in online mentions, followed by fashion at about 65 percent and alcohol brands at about 60 percent (you can draw your own conclusions on that last one).

Chapter 3

THE CASE FOR CUSTOMER EXPERIENCE

Many definitions of customer experience exist, but the one I prefer is "how customers feel about every single interaction with a brand." The definition has two core parts: "how customers feel" and "every single interaction."

How customers *feel* is important because perception is reality, so if a customer feels frustrated or angry or inconvenienced, then the experience needs to be improved. Remembering that every single interaction adds up to a holistic view of the company is also important because so many companies operate in silos and those silos make themselves apparent in disconnected customer experiences.

The customer experience bar is low, but the stakes are high, and the rewards are great.

The truth is, the bar for customer experience is very, very low. According to Acquia, "90% of customers believe that when it comes to delivering a good customer experience, most brands fail to meet their expectations." What's even more mindboggling is that "82% of marketers believe they *are* meeting customer expectations with regard to customer experience."[13] Clearly, there is a serious disconnect.

The same report found that customers want the following:

- 90 percent of customers want "a convenient experience" when they interact with a brand online.
- 68 percent of customers say, "My experience with brands online needs to be made easier."

- 💡 80 percent of customers say, "I would be more loyal to a brand that showed they really understood me and what I was looking for."[14]

But this is what customers get:

- 💡 66 percent of customers say, "When I engage with businesses online, I feel like I am treated as any other generic customer, not as an individual with my own needs."

- 💡 63 percent of customers say, "I often abandon a brand for another when the online experience is poor."

- 💡 72 percent of customers say, "I am loyal to certain brands, but as soon as I have a bad experience with them, I move on."[15]

Roughly half of customers say they would switch to a competitor after just one bad experience, according to Zendesk, a customer relationship management company. In the case of more than one bad experience, that number snowballs to 80 percent.[16]

Messaging platform Podium summarized the importance of customer experience well:

"Today's consumers are not the consumers of yesterday. They are more resourceful, selective, technological, and accustomed to convenience. More importantly, they are on the search for businesses who will actually listen to them and make genuine efforts to cater to their preferences and meet their needs. They are looking for personal relationships, trust, transparency, and communication."[17]

What about return on investment (ROI)?

InfoQuest, a provider of internet hosting and data center services, analyzed customer satisfaction data from the findings of more than 20,000 customer surveys conducted in forty countries. The conclusions of the study clearly established a link between customer satisfaction and revenue:

- 💡 A totally satisfied customer contributes 2.6 times as much revenue to a company as a somewhat satisfied customer.

- 💡 A totally satisfied customer contributes 14 times as much revenue as a somewhat dissatisfied customer.

- 💡 A totally dissatisfied customer decreases revenue at a rate equal to 1.8 times what a totally satisfied customer contributes to a business.[18]

In other words, satisfied customers create additional revenue, and dissatisfied customers create the "leaky bucket" that loses revenue at a faster pace.

Watermark Consulting looked at the Forrester Customer Experience Index, one of the major annual rankings about companies in almost every industry. Watermark focused on public companies only and compared stock returns of the customer experience leaders and laggards to the S&P 500 over an eleven-year period.

The leaders in customer experience returned 183.8 percent from 2007-2017, far outperforming the market (the S&P 500 Index returned 138.7 percent), while the laggards severely trailed the market with just a 63.1 percent return.[19]

What's most impressive is that the leader stocks returned nearly *three times* those of the laggards.

McKinsey & Company similarly found that "focusing on customer experience is a winning strategy in recession," as the top ten ranked publicly traded companies in the same Forrester Customer Experience Index outperformed the bottom ten by three times during the recession of 2007-2009.[20]

So if someone at work asks about the ROI of customer experience, show him or her any of the three reports just mentioned.

This applies to private companies too, since the biggest factor in long-term stock price is profitability. It also applies to B2B (business-to-business) companies. In fact, everything in this book applies to B2B companies, which often have even more opportunity because so few in the space are truly customer-focused.

Often, B2Bs have "customer success" departments, and GetFeedback, a customer experience feedback platform, aptly describes this team as "responsible for post-sales onboarding, adoption, and usage monitoring."[21]

With just one quick look at a job description for many "customer success" roles, it's clear that "customer success" is just a euphemism for "inside sales." If a customer success team is not incentivized on client satisfaction, willingness to recommend, or even success of the engagement, and if the team is held accountable solely for getting each client to renew and ideally spend more money next year than they did this year, then that is a sales department. It is not a customer experience department.

Unfortunately, that kind of strategy puts the company at odds with the very customer it is trying to retain *because that's not how clients think*. No matter how happy clients are with your SaaS (software-as-a-service) platform, they don't want to pay more next year; they want to pay *less*. Your job is to provide them with so much value that they can't live without your product or service. That will plug the "leaky bucket" and make price irrelevant.

The GetFeedback study found that "about six of 10 organizations have a Customer Success team, but that by itself was not a differentiator. What matters more: teamwork. Sixty-two percent of Leaders say that Customer Success and CX teams work well together, versus just 49% for Laggards."[22]

In fact, the study continues, most B2B businesses lack a core CX team, defined as "responsible for collecting customer feedback in coordinating CX activities with other departments." Forty-two percent of respondents did not have even one part-time person taking ownership for these CX activities.[23]

Let's say that again for emphasis: 42 percent of B2B businesses don't have even a single person focused squarely on customer experience. This is why there is so much opportunity for B2B companies.

Don't be distracted by the word "consumer" or "customer" in any of the research or case studies shared in this book. Remember that your clients are consumers in their "real life," and whether you like it or not, they are comparing you against the experiences they are having with consumer brands. If you run an e-commerce site, who do you think your customers are comparing it to? Likewise, your business clients are comparing the experience of working with you to every other experience they've had as a professional or a consumer.

Chapter 4

BECOMING WISE

W hat makes an experience remarkable or, literally, worthy of remark? After all, that's what word-of-mouth marketing is, right? It's getting your customers to talk about their experiences with their friends, family, and social media followers.

How does a company uncover experience opportunities across a vast array of communication channels, customer touchpoints, and corporate departments? Luckily, we don't need to solve all of those all at once. The key is getting some measurable customer experience wins that leave your customers—and your bosses—wanting more.

"Achieving customer experience 'perfection' is not an attainable goal—at least not in today's environment," says marketing research company eMarketer. "Companies must continue to chip away at complex efforts like obtaining a single customer view and an omni-channel one; they should also focus on some of the easier-to-execute aspects of customer experience like establishing core values, identifying the most commonly used channels and improving their email efforts."[24]

In other words, customer experience is a journey, not a destination.

I have developed a proprietary methodology for identifying and creating remarkable customer experiences. The four components aptly form the acronym WISE because when you execute them, your company will become "wise" to customer experience.

WISE stands for **Witty**, **Immersive**, **Shareable**, and **Extraordinary**.

We will review each of these components in detail, sharing a plethora of real-life examples of companies using these techniques to delight their customers. Their successes are meant to inspire you to do the same at your business—customized, of course, to your industry, company, and customer base.

The examples embody three characteristics that I always recommend companies strive for when creating customer experiences: They are simple, practical, and inexpensive.

Why those three characteristics? Customers crave experiences that are simple, and companies crave projects that don't take months or years to execute. A practical solution is one that solves some customer problem and can be implemented using existing company resources. And inexpensive—well, hopefully that one speaks for itself, because experience improvements that don't require big budgets are much more likely to be approved by management.

Not every experience needs to have all four components of WISE, and in fact it is very difficult to achieve all four in a single experience. That said, the more components that are incorporated into an experience, the more remarkable that experience will become. Even a single component will separate an experience from the rest of the *meh* experiences out there.

"The modern customer doesn't reward passable experiences—they want to be dazzled every time they interact with the brand," according to Brandwatch. "When it comes down to it, we're all in the business of wooing our customers with a stellar experience."[25]

Chapter 5

WITTY

L et's start with the first letter of WISE, which stands for Witty. Now, when I say Witty, I don't mean funny. I'm not talking about humor, because humor can be dangerous since it is different for different people. What I find funny you might find offensive or vice versa. So I'm not telling you to go out there and be a standup comedian with your brand. A very small number of brands—Taco Bell, Wendy's, Old Spice, and Charmin come to mind—can get away with humor as a defining aspect of their image. More than likely, though, you don't work for a brand like that.

Being Witty is a little bit different; it's more like being clever.

What I'm asking you to do is look at every piece of communication that you have and try to figure out how you can change the words to be a little bit more clever, to maybe put a smile on someone's face. So much of corporate communication, whether it's marketing, legal, digital, or something else, is *bor-ing*. It doesn't have to be, though. It's OK to have some fun with your customers and show some brand personality at the same time.

Signage, whether physical or digital, can play a large role in brand perception, yet too many companies don't give it much thought. A simple tweak can result in an entirely new message that is unique and memorable.

For example, look at this sign in downtown Manhattan that says, "We are probably the lowest priced in the city." I absolutely love this company, and I don't even know what it sells. Just from this sign, I know the people at this company have a personality. I know they're honest, and most importantly, I know I want to do business with them. It's the Stapleton Shoe Company, by the way, in case you were wondering, but it could have been anything.

This is a clever sign at a gas station right by my house: Gas is $2.99, but "Customer service is priceless!" Now if this gas station is across the street from another gas station selling gas at the same price, do you choose this one or the one selling 99-cent bottles of soda? I'm choosing this one because of just a couple of words on their sign that makes it feel like a more welcoming place. That's Witty.

I spotted another great sign outside a skyscraper in downtown Chicago. Two words—"Almost there . . ."—turn this otherwise unremarkable sign into one that's memorable. How long did it take to add those words to the sign? I know those little plastic letters are sometimes challenging to adhere, but maybe it took a couple of minutes to add those two words that turn this sign into something that is worthy of taking a picture. The person who spent the extra time to add just fourteen characters to this sign understood the power of words to make or break an experience. And the cost of being just a little bit friendlier was exactly nothing.

Similarly, at Philz Coffee, the "please wait" sign aimed at java enthusiasts waiting their turn to order added a touch of friendliness to make it stand out. What looks like a hand-drawn smiley face is accompanied by "You're up next! Hang tight." The casual language brings a sense of excitement for one's "turn" in line and also a sense of calm that it won't be a long wait.

Whenever you require your customers to wait, you risk frustrating them. After all, do you enjoy waiting on hold or in a long line? No one does. So that's the perfect opportunity to employ something Witty to take the customer's mind off of having to wait.

In the Louisville, Kentucky, airport, one of the first signs to appear on the walk toward baggage claim talks about "distilling great experiences." Not only is it telling you that you're going to have a terrific experience in Louisville, but it uses a play on words because, of course, Louisville is known for being home to the bourbon industry. The sign is clever. It is much better than just "Welcome to Louisville." It makes you stop for a minute and notice it.

Speaking of whiskey, this is a food truck in Boston. I had the honor of speaking to more than 1,400 people at the INBOUND marketing conference there, and for lunch the conference offered a unique experience: the choice to dine at more than two dozen food trucks offering a variety of culturally distinct dishes. The challenge? Determining which one to pick.

The psychology of choice plays a big role in our daily lives. According to *Psychologist World,* "The majority of decisions we make, such as which clothes to wear this morning or what to eat for lunch, are made routinely without substantial conscious consideration on our part."[26]

This is mostly because things like getting dressed or eating a meal fall at the bottom of psychologist Abraham Maslow's hierarchy of needs pyramid—namely, physiological needs that are essential to our survival.[27] In other words, deciding what we eat is less important than deciding that we need to eat.

So how did I choose among all those food trucks? As soon as I saw this sign, my mind was made up. Who wouldn't want to go to this food truck, no matter what kind of food they serve? It doesn't matter because you know that this is going to be a fun food truck. This is going to be a company that you want to do business with. By the way, I still paid with a credit card.

Even a simple door can be turned into a memorable experience. How much more memorable is this door ("Nothing to see here . . .") versus almost any other broom closet, utility room, or emergency exit door that you've ever seen? Someone had some fun with this door, and if it results in more people smiling (and, hopefully, following directions by not opening the door), then it's a win. While some may say that it invites investigation into what's behind it, I think the sign gives the passerby a brief chuckle that is more than worth the inability to solve the mystery.

Witty signs can show up in unexpected places.

Like virtually every other restaurant in the world, Sushi-san in Chicago (also owned by Lettuce Entertain You) has a sign directing patrons to the restrooms. But unlike most other restaurants in the world, Sushi-san does not use the international stick figure bathroom symbols on its sign.

Instead, the restaurant uses a lit-up sign featuring the ubiquitous "poop emoji." The sign says it all without using a single word.

Sticking with the bathroom theme, this sign was spotted in a UK bathroom: "Please don't flush nappies, sanitary towels, paper towels, gum, old phones, unpaid bills, junk mail, your ex's sweater, hopes, dreams or goldfish down this toilet."

See how it got the point across—we've all seen similar signs like this in bathrooms—while also having some fun and causing a little bit of laughter in an unexpected place? That's how easy it is to create a remarkable customer experience using the Witty technique.

Image: Michael Pace. Used with permission.

Some companies have added wittiness to their product offerings.

For example, bubly™ Sparkling Water, a product of PepsiCo, added fun messages to its cans—a different one for each flavor. According to the press release at the product launch in 2018:

> *Each bubly flavor features bright, bold packaging, unique smiles for every flavor, and comes with its own Witty greeting on the tab (like "Hey u," "hiii," and "yo") and personal messages on the can (such as "I feel like I can be open around u," "hold cans with me," and "love at first phssst"), for maximum enjoyment and smiles.*[28]

The first thing most consumers notice is the greeting on the tab because it is strategically placed right where their finger goes to open the can. The fact that each flavor has a different message definitely elicits a smile. The beauty of the campaign? It succeeds in establishing a humanlike relationship between the consumer and . . . a can of sparkling water.

It's also brilliant in its simplicity. After all, it's just a few words atop or on the side of a can that already had other printing on it. It's clever, memorable, and shows off the brand's personality. A friend pointed out that the tab messages replaced the standard hole that apparently—though I had never heard of this—was meant for a straw. So that must have required a minor production change, but it was well worth the investment. In fact, PepsiCo CEO Ramon Laguarta told analysts in July 2019 that bubly "is going to be one of our next billion-dollar brands."[29]

BUBLY, the Bubly Designs and the Bubly Marks are trademarks. Used with permission.

☆ ☆ ☆ ☆ ☆

The back of Conagra's Manwich® Bold Sloppy Joe Sauce cans include four simple instructions for preparation that are also Witty:

1. Cook 1 lb. of meat (thoroughly)
2. Add Manwich sauce!!!!
3. Ask to be called Chef to anyone who addresses you
4. Serve, dig in, & leave hunger behind

I literally laughed out loud when I read the part about asking to be called "Chef," and then of course I asked my kids to refer to me as Chef for the rest of the evening. Also, four exclamation points is just great. The experience difference between these fun cooking instructions and a typical recipe is immense, yet the cost or effort to make the change was minimal. You want to strive for these kind of experience changes in your business.

One last food example in case you are still hungry: My good friend Heath Schecter, who actually is a chef (and author of *i'm a chef & my kids want buttered noodles: a collection of recipes*), likes to play around with unexpected food pairings that show off his sense of humor. Coming from a Jewish background, he has a particular affinity for mixing typical Jewish food with atypical nonkosher ingredients. One favorite? Bacon-wrapped matzo balls. You can bet they always get a laugh from both the Jewish and non-Jewish crowds, and in case you are wondering, they are *geshmak* (Yiddish for "delicious").

ASOS is a UK fashion brand. The company printed a packaging bag that had a mistake on it. (Do you see it?) Most companies would have not noticed the mistake or, if they had, would have thrown out the bags. But not ASOS. They turned the mistake into marketing gold by creating a self-deprecating social media post. That Witty tweet got them nearly 50,000 likes and nearly 8,600 retweets, plus countless new admirers. When is the last time your social media marketing team accomplished that?

This wasn't hard. This didn't cost any money. (In fact, not throwing away the bags saved money!) By taking an extra minute to think about what they could do to be just a little bit different, they got people talking, including many people who probably had never heard of ASOS or weren't customers. Now these people are introduced to the company for the first time and they immediately like it; they can already tell doing business with this company is going to be fun.

What would have happened if you or your company had made that same printing error? Can you admit when you make a mistake and can you be self-deprecating about it? After all, we're all human; we all make mistakes, and it's OK to laugh at ourselves about it. Acknowledging that can create a lasting connection with your customers. What ASOS did was Witty, authentic, memorable, and—based on the social media response—eminently remarkable.

☆ ☆ ☆ ☆ ☆

Drizly is a liquor delivery service, and it too made a somewhat embarrassing mistake. The company sent an email with the subject line, "Let's get this party started, {name}." Now anyone who has ever sent an email campaign knows that "{name}" refers to a "merge tag" which *should* have substituted each recipient's first name instead of displaying the tag by itself.

That alone isn't such a big deal, only because we've all seen that happen before. But unfortunately, the inside of the email says "Things just got personal" and then includes a list of "Recommendations for you"—all of which had greyed-out photos. "Lorem ipsum" appeared instead of product names (*Lorem ipsum* is placeholder text, often referred to as "Greek" even though it's a corrupted form of Latin), and "From $XX.XX" appeared instead of real prices!

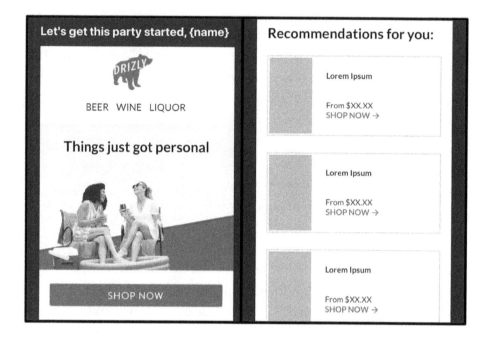

This probably wasn't as "personal" as Drizly had intended.

The company more than redeemed itself, though, with its self-deprecating response—a second email with the subject line, "lol, wtf was that." The email read:

> You might've gotten an email from us earlier today that was, let's call it "incomplete." It likely referred to you as "{name}" and offered you a bunch of "personalized" picks that were just a bunch of lorem ipsum text and xxx's.
>
> Here at Drizly, we're all about accepting responsibility for both our triumphs and our shortcomings. So here's what happened:
>
> My dog did it.
>
> And if you don't believe that incredibly true story and think we just messed up, well use promo code LOREMIPSUM for $5 off or FREE delivery on your next order. Thanks for your understanding.

lol, wtf was that.

You might've gotten an email from us earlier today that was, let's call it "incomplete." It likely referred to you as "{name}" and offered you a bunch of "personalized" picks that were just a bunch of lorem ipsum text and xxx's.

Here at Drizly, we're all about accepting responsibility for both our triumphs and our shortcomings. So here's what happened:

My dog did it.

And if you don't believe that incredibly true story and think we just messed up, well, use promo code LOREMIPSUM for $5 OFF or FREE delivery on your next order (valid 5/18-5/24). Thanks for your understanding.

*Must be 21+ to order in the USA or 18+/19+ in Canada depending on provincial law. Promo code valid until May 24th at 11:59pm PST. Codes may be applied to the delivery fees or products, depending on applicable state or provincial laws. Promos are not valid in CT, MO, OH, or HI. Discounts are restricted to delivery fees in IN, MA, ME, MN, NC, NJ, TX, VA, WA and Alberta. Codes cannot be combined with any other offers. Not valid at all retailers. Items are subject to availability and may not be carried by all retailers. Prices are set by retailers in your area. Input your delivery address on www.drizly.com or on our apps for local inventory and pricing information.

What's brilliant about this response? The company got out in front of the mistake, acknowledged it, poked fun at itself, and included a nice bonus offer as a make-good (with a Witty promo code). Suffice it to say, none of Drizly's customers was upset about the error, and they probably liked the company even more after the mistake.

☆ ☆ ☆ ☆ ☆

Recently, I received a travel magazine in the mail from the state of Nebraska. Normally, I wouldn't have given much thought to it, but I was drawn to the photo on the cover. I'm not entirely sure what's going on in the photo, but it looks like a family paddling down a river in a metal bathtub.

Looking closer, I noticed the small subheading above the "Visit Nebraska" title. It read, "The Official 2019 Not-At-All-What-You-Thought Nebraska State Travel Guide." Witty, right? It got me thinking about my thoughts about Nebraska and what could be inside that was not what I was thinking about. It was just enough to pique my interest in the guidebook when normally the book would have immediately ended up in the recycling bin.

The best part of the magazine cover was at the bottom, where you really had to be paying attention. Underneath the word "Nebraska" in that little outline of the state, it said, "Honestly, it's not for everyone."

Who wants to go to Nebraska now? Everyone.

The lesson here? It's OK to ask the question of who is *not* your customer or what product or service is *not* for your customer because if we try to sell stuff to people that they don't want, we lose credibility. Instead, if we're able to say, you know what, this customer probably isn't the right target for this product, we're actually helping them. We're doing them a favor, and we're gaining trust plus a positive reflection on the brand.

Why is that important if the person wasn't going to be our customer in the first place? Because they may know people who are indeed our target customers, and they can still help us out with some word-of-mouth marketing.

What's more, we're doing our sales team a favor by identifying people they don't need to waste time contacting since they aren't going to buy from us anyway. This helps them be more efficient and effective. I once had a salesperson call me so many times and leave countless voicemails. I finally picked up one day just to tell him that I wasn't interested. Just like that, it seemed that a huge weight rose from his shoulders. He thanked me because he could now cross my name off his list and not waste any more time with me!

B2B Examples

B2B readers, I haven't forgotten about you. And although the B2C examples above could all be engineered within the B2B environment as well, I also wanted to include some B2B examples to prove that this is easily doable in the B2B space.

Anybody that uses Slack, the business communication platform, is greeted with a Witty welcome message when they open the software. It says, "Please enjoy Slack responsibly." It's not supposed to make you laugh out loud, but it's a clever play on the beer, wine, and liquor advertisements, which include "Please enjoy responsibly" in the legally mandated disclaimer language at the bottom.

If it gets people to start their day with a smile, it's a win for the product.

Please enjoy Slack responsibly.

- Your friends at Slack

It also conveys that the Slack brand has a personality. It's a fun company, one with which it is enjoyable to do business. Incidentally, Slack also lets administrators add their own personalized welcome messages, which can be rotated on a daily basis to inspire or inform employees as they start their day.

When I first met fellow speaker and business coach Marquesa Pettway, I knew I was going to like her. Marquesa's effervescent personality and joyful enthusiasm for helping others was immediately contagious. Her Speakerpreneur™ training helped me develop The Experience Maker™ brand and its related offerings.

On Marquesa's website, there's an engaging picture of her and an encouraging message: "Let's do this!" But what immediately stood out to me was the call-to-action button at the bottom, which reads: "Login Darlin.'"

If you know Marquesa, you know that "Login Darlin'" is perfectly on brand for her. It communicates so much in one extra word about who Marquesa is and what it's like to work with her. She's fun, she's friendly, and she's got personality. Did it cost her any more to add a word to her login button? Of course not, but its value to the overall client experience is priceless.

Now that you've scrolled all the way to the bottom...

It's just the right time to stop reading and do some clicking instead.

I want to learn more, Book a Demo

Planable, a crowd-sourced planning platform acquired by a company called Connectus, had a typical page on its website detailing each of its paid plans. There was a list of features and benefits, comparisons of what came with each plan, some testimonials, and a lot of scrolling.

What was atypical appeared at the very bottom of the page: a humorous headline with a call-to-action button. "Now that you've scrolled all the way to the bottom . . .," it read, "It's just the right time to stop reading and do some clicking instead."

What a clever way to get someone's attention who has clearly spent a decent amount of time on the website!

You probably have a website where there's a lot of text and scrolling. But does it lead to anything? Is there any payoff for scrolling all the way down to the bottom like there was on Planable's site?

This reminded me of watching a movie and waiting all the way to the end of the credits for that extra scene. This is an easy thing to do on your website, no matter what business you're in.

None of these Witty examples is complicated or expensive. Most are just friendlier and quirkier than what we would expect, and that exceeding of expectations is exactly what makes a remarkable customer experience.

Where can you change the language your company uses in front of customers? Even if you don't have a physical storefront, there are countless opportunities to surprise your customers with friendlier language in communications. Consider:

- Marketing: email, direct mail, social media, display ads, search ads, website and mobile app promotions, billboards, package inserts
- Customer Service: telephone, email and chat scripts, social media and messaging interactions
- Product: packaging, software platforms, website content, user experience
- Servicing: contracts, statements of work, welcome letters, invoices, user manuals, FAQs

Next time you're writing anything that a customer will see, have a marketer or just a funny colleague take a look to see if you too can change a few words to transform a typical experience into a memorable one.

Chapter 6

IMMERSIVE

Now that we've learned about all the places where we can be Witty, let's talk about being Immersive. Being Immersive means looking at the entire customer journey and ensuring that it makes sense as a whole. The entire experience should be one continuous smooth ride that your customers *feel*.

Chances are you've heard (or even uttered) the word "silo" at your company. So many businesses are siloed, meaning that the organizational structure creates lots of different teams that are in charge of different parts of the customer experience. These teams have names like acquisition, usage, and retention; in a B2B company they might be called sales and customer success.

The problem is that siloed businesses create siloed experiences because every department owns a different part of the experience and the departments often don't communicate with each other. They create the best experiences they can, but the poor customer is left with really awkward, inconsistent, or disjointed transitions between experiences.

Research company eMarketer calls "lack of single ownership for omnichannel efforts" a "big problem" in customer experience.

"Everyone must align on the overarching goals and visions of delivering the experience," eMarketer adds.[30]

GetFeedback found that the top obstacle for B2B companies is also silos within the organization. Like their B2C counterparts, the issue is largely a factor of a company's size: 33 percent for small, 57 percent for medium, and 73 percent for large enterprises.

In other words, "as organizations get bigger, delivering a good end-to-end journey becomes more challenging."[31]

According to Zendesk, 70 percent of customers expect companies to collaborate on their behalf, and 68 percent of customers are annoyed when their call is transferred between departments.[32]

Being Immersive means delivering a consistent, connected experience so that the whole thing feels right to the customer.

One way to accomplish this is to always ask where the customer came from before they arrived at this part of the experience and where are they going next. Then make sure that those transitions are smooth.

An Immersive experience takes all that into consideration and is a journey that remains consistently smooth.

It also helps to get customers feeling the experience more deeply.

If you have kids, you've probably seen *The Greatest Showman*, and if you haven't, please put this book down and go watch it right now (but don't forget to come back!). It is a terrific movie with great music and a positive message. I highly recommend it.

If you have a young daughter, you've undoubtedly seen *Frozen*—also a terrific movie with great music and positive messages.

These movies have one other thing in common, which has remained rare in the movie industry: After a successful first run in theaters, they came back for a second run. The second time, though, they were billed as "singalong" versions.

Think about the typical experience of going to a movie theater. You're told to be quiet and not talk. You're told to turn off your phone. Basically you're just supposed to sit there and silently watch the movie.

Now think about this singalong experience. This time, you can stand up and belt out song lyrics with the movie characters, with everyone else in the theater doing the same thing. What an Immersive experience!

These films took a typical moviegoing experience and shifted it to be so Immersive that viewers felt it in their bones. For those like me that had these soundtracks running in the house 24/7 so that we all knew every word to every song, that created a memorable and lasting experience.

Is it any surprise that two of my daughter's favorite movies are *The Greatest Showman* and *Frozen*?

BT is a British telecommunications company that understands that one of the most confusing parts about becoming a customer is the first bill. You have probably experienced this at least once; you get that first bill and it's got some partial month charges from last month and some other charge for this month, and maybe a prepayment for next month's charges, and then a bunch of one-time setup fees. It's like $400, and the first thing you're thinking is, *What have I gotten myself into? I thought this was a special promotion.*

BT decided to create a video that has two employees explaining all of the elements of the first bill. But to make it Immersive, the company went a step further by infusing it with technology that incorporates *your bill* into the video. So when those employees show you a charge in the video, it's actually your charge and not just a generic example. Brilliant!

Here is the transcription of a sample video. Pay attention to how the actors take care to simplify everything about this normally complex experience:

> *[Woman] Hello, Caroline. We're from BT. It's really good to have you with us, and we're going to talk you through your first bill. Your bill is made up of three sections: One-off charges, rental and other charges, and what you used.*
>
> *[Man] Let's start at the top. One-off charges include things like delivery, an engineer connecting your line, activation fees, and any new kit you needed to get set up. And this is what that section comes to. [Man shows a tablet screen that says "Caroline Wilcox" at the top and the "One-off charges: £36.50."]*
>
> *The next section is rental and other charges. This is the cost of all the services you have with us, including any discounts. It's billed in advance and comes to this. [Tablet screen shows Caroline's name*

and then "Rental & other charges: £29.99" and lists three bulleted charges of "Line Rental," "BT Sport," and "AMC."]

[Woman] Now, for the last part, what you used. This covers anything you've used over and above your package, things like calls to international numbers or buying a film perhaps. And for you, this month that comes to this. [Tablet screen shows Caroline's name and "What you used: £3.49."]

[Man] So if we now put those three sections together, you'll get the total for your first bill. [Tablet screen again shows Caroline's name and "Your first bill: £69.98" along with the subtotals of the three sections.]

And that's how it all works. We hope that's been a help, and everything makes sense now.

[Woman] If you want to see your bill in more detail, just click on the button at the end of the film. You'll find it's all there for you. Thanks for watching.

One of the best and easiest ways to improve the customer experience is to find the customer pain points, difficulties, or confusion, and then alleviate them. Short of that, being willing to explain confusing parts of the journey, like BT did, will go a long way toward keeping customers happy.

In your business, it might be an application, contract, user agreement, onboarding process, billing statement, or something else that is prone to cause confusion. If you can't make it simpler, at least try to explain it to your customers or clients.

More than that, though, doing this will save your company money. If customers can finally understand their first bill, maybe they'll stop calling customer service for an explanation. That can result in huge cost savings while also creating a unique and remarkable experience that people want to talk about with friends and family.

When did you last look at your company's invoices? Are they clear? Do customers understand the charges? What about contracts and statements of work or even sales brochures? If you are asking a customer to interpret information from your company, are you being as clear and concise as you can?

☆ ☆ ☆ ☆ ☆

When customers order a pizza for delivery, one common fear is that the order is going to be wrong. This is because the pizza-making process is a "blind" part of the customer experience; customers don't get to witness it so they have to just believe in the process. (Other similar examples are a dentist telling you a tooth needs a crown or an auto mechanic saying you need new brakes; most of us aren't knowledgeable enough to argue, so we have to take it on faith that the providers are honest and good at their jobs.)

So we order a pizza with our favorite toppings, wait a half hour or more for the pizza to arrive, tip the driver generously (I was a pizza delivery boy for Domino's in my youth), and . . . hope that the right toppings are on the pizza.

What if a company developed a way to remove this fear? Wouldn't that greatly enhance the overall experience? Well, Domino's did just that with what they call "delivery insurance," which is actually a follow-up to an initial concept called "carryout insurance."

Offering "Free protection for your most delicious asset," carryout insurance launched with a thirty-second TV commercial that hilariously explored all the ways a pizza could be ruined on the way home, including canine interference and a guy on a scooter running over the box.

"Just bring it back and we'll remake it for free," the ad promised.[33]

The accompanying website maintained the same humorous tone and offered even more examples under a headline that read, "Yeah, we cover that." Examples included "I slipped on something slippery," "I braked. It flew," and "I tripped on a sprinkler."[34]

Delivery insurance was a logical follow-up, though without the same fanfare.

"When you place your Domino's delivery order, you also place your trust in the brand. Domino's stores do everything they can to make sure their pizza experts create your meal exactly the way you want it, with piping hot goodness delivered right to your door. Domino's Delivery Insurance Program provides extra peace of mind," according to the website.[35]

Did Domino's suddenly become an insurance company? Of course not; they're simply saying what they've always said—that your satisfaction is guaranteed—in a different and memorable way. If you don't get the pizza you want or you don't like the pizza, they'll make a new one for you with no questions asked.

Domino's successfully tapped into the human emotions during the customer journey of ordering a pizza, which is why it's Immersive. They get bonus points for also being Witty!

I recalled two specific pizza delivery memories when I read about delivery insurance.

The first memory involved a guy who always ordered the same thing, and none of the drivers ever wanted to deliver his order. Why? Because it was a small triple anchovy pizza, and if you did not drive with your windows down even in the winter, your car smelled like anchovies for the next three weeks.

The second memory involved a guy who always ordered the same thing, and every one of the drivers wanted to deliver his order. Why? Because that large pepperoni and sausage pizza belonged to His Airness himself, Michael Jordan! I was lucky enough to deliver to him once; he answered the door in a white T-shirt and basketball shorts and looked over my head not just because he is very tall but likely because he was looking for uninvited guests.

The other drivers had prepped me, telling me that if I asked for an autograph, I'd get one but not a tip, or I could take the cash. At that moment, I decided the man deserved his privacy, so I took the very generous tip. Even as a teenager, I was thinking of the customer!

☆ ☆ ☆ ☆ ☆

Against the Grain is a smokehouse and brewery in Louisville, Kentucky, located just outside Louisville Slugger Field—home to the Louisville Bats, a Minor League Baseball team. Among the many humorously named cocktails on the menu, including "Too Many Exes" and "Pig on Vacation," is a drink that any self-respecting customer experience practitioner couldn't help but try: the "Old Fashioned Experience."

Described as "a house-made ice sphere containing all the ingredients of an Old Fashioned, paired with Michter's expressions [bourbon, rye, sour mash, or American whiskey]," the drink arrives as a glass with a large ice sphere inside and a double shot of whiskey on the side.

The ice ball almost looks like a detached eyeball with a "bloody" maraschino cherry frozen inside, along with a splash of bitters and an orange peel. (Through experimentation at home, I learned that the ball also likely contains something like Cointreau, an orange liqueur generically known as triple sec. Triple sec prevents the ball from freezing solid; the result is a solid structure with more of a slushy interior. This is important because of how the "experience" of the drink evolves.)

When the whiskey (I chose bourbon as I was in Kentucky, after all) is poured over the ice sphere, it causes the ice to begin slowly melting. As it melts, the frozen ingredients of the old-fashioned mix with the alcohol, turning the drink into an old-fashioned in front of the customer's eyes. It's a constantly progressing "experience" that affects at least three of the senses—sight, smell, and taste—at the same time. Importantly, it's much more memorable than a standard old-fashioned.

You can't get much more Immersive than IKEA did in a printed advertisement that ran only in Europe. In what just may be the best ad headline ever, IKEA began with: "Peeing on this ad may change your life."

Developed by the Åkestam Holst agency in Sweden, the ad showed a large picture of a crib and a white strip at the bottom that was made from the same chemical as an at-home pregnancy test. The idea was that if a woman wanted to find out if she was pregnant, she could pee on the ad.

If she was indeed pregnant, the ad didn't show a pink or blue plus or minus sign. Instead, it showed a 50 percent off your crib coupon! Amazing, right?

What I want you to take from the IKEA ad is not that you should ask people to pee on your advertisements too but rather that you should always ask, "What if?"

What if we did something totally crazy and out there? What if we did something that no one else has ever done? What if we did something that everyone says can't be done?

Somebody at IKEA or Åkestam Holst asked "What if?" and the rest is history. Not surprisingly, IKEA got so much press for the advertisement and so many people sharing it that I'd bet the earned media far outweighed the paid media for the campaign.

Speaking of peeing, the urinals inside the *USS Midway* Museum in San Diego have green mats on the bottom, a plastic soccer goal, and a miniature soccer ball that hangs on a string and moves when you . . . well, I think you get the idea, and I'd like to keep this a family-friendly book.

In all seriousness, though, if someone can create an experience out of a urinal, don't you think that you can create a memorable experience in your business?

There's a great little company based in San Francisco called Imperfect Foods (formerly Imperfect Produce). I absolutely love this company, and it could really fit into every part of the WISE framework, but I'm filing it under Immersive because the entire customer experience is so fluid and consistent.

The company's mission is to "eliminate food waste and build a better food system for everyone."[36] It does so by boxing up excess, misshapen, oddly sized, and off-spec produce and grocery items into weekly subscription boxes delivered to each customer's doorstep.

The food is perfectly edible and delicious and is usually offered at below-market prices. There's nothing wrong with the food, but supermarkets have strict cosmetic standards for produce and that which doesn't measure up usually ends up in a landfill.

Fun marketing messages appear throughout the customer journey, starting with this billboard spotted in Chicago: "We'll help you get dates." Both the play on words and the clever images of fruit (and vegetables) with googly eyes are pervasive throughout every piece of communication.

The delivery box is filled with fun and useful messages, from produce storage instructions to stories about the unglamorous existence of a heart-shaped potato to a funny note on the bottom of the box. (I won't ruin the surprise.)

When did you last turn a cardboard box around and around to make sure you looked at every single panel, even the bottom? Imperfect Foods makes it so you almost have to.

A personalized tracker on the website makes the experience more Immersive by telling each customer their contribution to reducing landfill waste, saving water, and eliminating carbon dioxide emissions. When customers hit certain milestones, they get a surprise note and small gift like a reusable grocery bag in their next box. The recurring enforcement and celebration of success encourages customer retention because it reaffirms the choice to buy from Imperfect Foods and support the planet.

The company also encourages people to take pictures of their misshapen fruit and vegetables and share them. I happened to find a heart-shaped potato that perfectly matched the one on the box. So naturally I shared a photo of me holding it on Instagram.

Case Study: Benco Dental

Tucked away in an industrial park in Pittston, Pennsylvania (about two and a half hours northwest of Philadelphia), up a long driveway, past a large sculpture of a tooth, sits Benco Dental. Benco is the largest privately owned dental equipment and supplies distributor in the United States. Inside, among the corporate offices and the hundreds of historical dentistry artifacts from the owner's personal collection, sits CenterPoint Design, home to an incredibly Immersive experience for Benco's dental customers.

CenterPoint is a showroom featuring twenty-five fully equipped dental operatories. That's the little room patients go into to get their teeth cleaned or for other dental procedures. Dentists are invited to spend a day touring the facility to get design ideas and inspiration for their own dental offices, whether they are just starting out or perhaps redesigning an existing practice.

Melissa Sprau is director of design at Benco Dental, and she led me on the same tour she gives to dozens of dentists each year (Benco is a consulting client of mine).

"Welcome to CenterPoint. We're so glad that you're here and that you made the trip," she began. "Believe it or not, here in little Pittston, Pennsylvania, we actually have the largest dental equipment showroom in the world."

Each of the operatories is filled with real dental equipment and supplies in order to replicate actual working conditions and help the dentists envision what a final design might look like.

"We have our operatories set up in lots of different ways. You might even notice some redundancies in the equipment and the delivery systems. There's more than what you might need in your typical work day in each operatory," Sprau explained. "We do this on purpose. We do this so that you can get in and get comfortable and position the equipment in exactly the way that you want to work. We want you to try it as if it's your own and really experience all of the different manufacturers, all of the different ways that you can set up a room, so that you leave here today feeling confident about the purchase that you're going to make."

That purchase just might be the biggest purchase a dentist makes for his or her practice, which is why Benco wants to ensure that its clients are completely comfortable with the design before making the decision to buy. Benco sells everything in the operatory, from the flooring tile to the box of exam gloves on the counter. Since every dentist is different, the showroom is meant to display all sorts of concepts in a flexible manner that allows for mixing and matching.

"To [the] patient, every operatory might look the same. They come in, they sit down in the chair, there's a light overhead," Sprau explained. "But to you as the dentist, you've got a lot of decisions to make. In addition to just the nuts and bolts of the equipment and where it's placed and how it affects your workflow, there's also flooring, wall covering, ambient lighting and task lighting—all of these different elements to consider."

Sprau added that the different operatories explore "different approaches and really get you thinking bigger and thinking differently, and to show you all of the possibilities of the total aesthetic of the operatory, in addition to the functional elements of the operatory equipment."

In other words, the experience covers both form and function.

A stop at the design library allows the dentist to peruse hundreds of flooring samples, everything from carpet to vinyl tile to porcelain. There are also tons of wall coverings, ranging from fancy to fanciful, from upscale to made for kids. Everything is prequalified as appropriate for a commercial healthcare environment.

If a dentist doesn't see exactly the right design for their needs, Benco has a solution for that as well—the Sandbox. A bunch of nondescript white boxes represent dental equipment, and the dentist can change the sizes and wheel them around to place them in exactly the right spot to create the "ideal" operatory space.

"When we're all done and you have everything placed exactly where you like, look up, there's a GoPro that's hanging from the ceiling," Sprau explained. "It's going to capture an image of the operatory layout that we've designed together so you know exactly the way you want to plan your space."

Remarkably, Benco provides this experience free of charge, including travel, to dentists who they know are looking to design or redesign an office. Why do they invest all this time, effort, and money into prospective customers who may not even end up buying? Because they know that customer experience is their true differentiator.

"We're not just trying to make a one-time big purchase and walk away," said Sprau. "We care about their long-term health and their long-term success as a business, and we want to give them the tools to support that. We make these deeper-level connections with customers, where we're not just talking about how many operatories and what color to paint the walls. We're talking about, 'What do you want your patients to feel when they come in and what do you want them to remember when they leave?' Or 'Doctor, what do you want to do to differentiate yourself from the practice up the street? What makes you love what you do and how can we help show that to the world through the design of your practice?'"

The result? Most dentists, after immersing themselves in the CenterPoint experience, go from thinking they might want to create a new office design to knowing they have to in order to stay modern and relevant. When they're ready, Benco's team of commercial interior designers will help them sketch out the entire office, up to and including where those boxes of gloves go.[37]

☆ ☆ ☆ ☆ ☆

Romance novelist Allie Pleiter has published more than forty books, releasing an average of four novels per year. She has sold more than 1.4 million books around the world, with titles like *My So-Called Love Life* and *The Lawman's Oklahoma Sweetheart.*

Now you're probably wondering what romance novels have to do with customer experience, and in particular, being Immersive in business. Well, a common recommendation in CX is to "walk in your customer's shoes." In fact, I always recommend to executives that they become a customer of their own company. It is the single best way to understand and appreciate how customers perceive doing business with you.

Pleiter does something similar as part of her writing routine: She puts herself in the shoes of her fictional characters.

"My primary customer experience is what a reader experiences when he or she reads one of my novels," Pleiter said. "I go out of my way to make sure that that experience is as rich and engrossing and enthralling as possible. Now, for me, that means that I need to do whatever I can to actually experience what I want my reader to experience. That's not only a good customer experience, it's also a lot of fun for me. I've had a lot of tremendously fun adventures doing it."

In other words, Pleiter experiences what her fictional characters experience before she writes about them. It's her way of adding authenticity to the characters' stories. What's remarkable is the list of experiences she's personally gone through in the name of "research":

> *I have talked to a circus and gone up onto a trapeze to get an idea of what that feels like. I've learned to work a ten-foot bullwhip because I needed a character who used a whip as one of his weapons. That was an amazing experience. I've had a world-class barista show me how to work one of the most expensive and intricate coffee machines . . .*
>
> *One of my favorites recently was I was working on a book that involved a bison ranch. I had the opportunity to spend a couple of days on the bison ranch, and they staged a bison stampede for me so that I got to feel like what it was like to be in the middle of a hundred 2,000-pound animals coming at you. Not only is that fun for me, and I think it shows up in the work—the fun that I'm having*

and the adventure that I'm not only going on but I'm pulling my reader on—but I think it makes for really vivid descriptions.

It has a chance to bring a reader along with me and create a really visceral, emotional, wonderful experience for them as they read one of my books. That's certainly what I hope happens, and I certainly have a tremendous amount of fun while I do it.[38]

If more businesses had their employees put themselves in the shoes of the customer like Pleiter does with her fictional characters, they too could "create a really visceral, emotional, wonderful experience for them."

Fresh Scents Inc., a leader in the "ambient marketing" industry, provides nursing homes, schools, hospitals, gyms, office buildings, hotels, and other entities with "scenting solutions" that are controlled by machines connected to mobile apps.

The company's website notes that "our sense of smell is so closely linked to memory, a pleasing aroma experience, or a bad one, can have lasting effects on a business' bottom line." What's more, the site says, "Retailers and business owners have come to realize that fragrance and odor control is an important branding factor that can't be ignored. Scent marketing has proven to attract new customers, increase the time customers linger in environments, create a branded, heightened value perception, encourage repeat visits, increase sales and inspire loyalty."[39]

I will admit that I hadn't thought much about "ambient marketing" as a contributing factor to customer experience until I met Naftuly Kraus at a conference at which I was speaking. Kraus—"Tuli" to his friends—describes himself in his LinkedIn profile as "The Scent Guy." I asked him to expound upon the power of scent in the customer experience.

"When you walk into a store and it smells amazing, you will have a better time at the store," he said. "You might even buy more products. You will be more relaxed, happy. But imagine you walked into the local retail shop and it smelled really bad. You will walk right back out of there. You might even tell your friends how bad your experience was."[40]

Kraus referenced a study by Wheeling Jesuit University that asked volunteers to sniff peppermint oil every two hours for five days. The peppermint sniffers were not as hungry during the week and ate an average of 2,800 fewer calories in a week.[41]

"There is a reason why these big hotel chains use great fragrances in the public areas," Kraus said. "I have friends that have come to me and said, 'Tuli, have you ever been to this hotel in, for example, Colorado?' I said, 'No,' and they tell me, 'They have this amazing fragrance, and it smells so good,' and I'm like, 'Do you go there often?' and they're like, 'I was there once a couple of years ago.' This just gives you an example [of] how far deep in your brain the sense of smell can be stuck if it's a good fragrance."[42]

Kraus gave me a small vial of a liquid scent that I immediately recalled smelling in a major high-end hotel chain. It turns out they're not the only hotel chain that has their own smell.

I found this concept to be absolutely fascinating, so I decided to research it a little bit more.

According to *Psychology Today*, olfaction, or the sense of smell, is the most primal of our six senses. Throughout human evolution, the sense of smell has been key to our survival: A negative smell, such as a dead animal, can trigger an instantaneous reflex to take flight, whereas a positive smell, such as burning wood or baking cookies, can trigger a sense of security. Humans are capable of distinguishing thousands of unique scents, and smell directly ties to memories in a way that no other sense can.[43]

Maybe WWE superstar-turned-actor Dwayne "The Rock" Johnson was actually onto something when he yelled his signature question, "Do you smell-l-l-l-l-l-l-l-l what The Rock is cooking?"

We know from the definition of customer experience that every interaction with a brand affects the overall experience perception, but this was the first time I had contemplated olfactory interactions. As I thought about it more, though, several examples emerged from everyday life:

An Uber or Lyft car with a really heavy air freshener or cigarette smell creates the urge to immediately roll down the windows.

Any Starbucks in the world has that same pleasant smell of coffee beans and baked goods that's really comforting. I believe that if I walked into a Starbucks blindfolded, I could probably tell you that I was in a Starbucks.

A real estate open house may feature freshly baked chocolate chip cookies because the broker knows that smell is really well received.

Brands like Auntie Anne's and Cinnabon are instantly identifiable by their scent, even several hundred feet away.

A hospital features a smell of antiseptic cleaning chemicals.

While smell may not be a part of every company's customer experience, you should at least consider it, especially if you are a business that has a physical presence. What are you doing to make sure that your brand not only looks good but smells good?

☆ ☆ ☆ ☆ ☆

JP Morgan Chase is the largest bank in the United States by assets, according to *Business Insider*,[44] so one of its challenges is competing with the thousands of small local banks that know their customers by name and can provide a more personalized experience.

Chase embarked on a project to display customized photography on its bank account login page to create a feeling of being localized. Depending on a user's ZIP code, a different background image automatically appears on the bank's login page.

Interestingly, all of the images are of neighborhoods, not of well-known locations. So with a San Francisco ZIP code, the image isn't of the Golden Gate Bridge; rather, it is of a local neighborhood that, presumably, only local residents would recognize. A Chicago ZIP code displays a couple walking underneath a random "L" train station; it doesn't show the Willis Tower or Navy Pier or any of Chicago's other iconic sites.

Chase went a step further by adding a time indicator to the URLs, recognizing whether it was daytime or nighttime when the user is logging in. The result is a different neighborhood photo that is taken either in the daytime or at night.

The customized photographs are fun and generally cause the user to stop for a moment to view (and hopefully appreciate) the image. They create a subconscious familiarity and connection with the bank, and we know that as humans we are all looking to feel a connection.

What's most impressive is Chase's ability to do it at a massive scale, although the fact that it's a digital experience makes that significantly easier.

From a marketing perspective, it gives the bank a unique look; when a user arrives at the website and sees a beautiful local image as a background, it's not what they would necessarily expect from a financial institution. It serves as a subtle reminder that they are banking with somebody different.

Every bank has an image of some sort on its website, but why can't that be a point of differentiation? Every experience can be enhanced with a little creativity.

The Chase experience also works because it is personalized. Personalization and customization can help customers feel closer to the brand. It makes them feel that you're listening to them and that you know them; it also builds trust. As one of my friends likes to say, "We are all in the trust business."

According to a report from Acquia, "Customers make no secret of what they expect: a convenient, personalized experience."[45]

Today's customers, whether they be consumers of a large bank or corporate clients of a SaaS (software-as-a-service) company, expect to be treated like more than an account number.

Acquia found that brands in general are not meeting customer needs for personalization:

- 💡 60 percent of customers agree with the statement, "I often feel that brands who should know me, don't know me very well."
- 💡 60 percent of customers agree with the statement, "Brands do not do a good job using my personal preferences to predict my needs."[46]

What's the payoff for a personalized experience? Customer loyalty.

- 💡 76 percent of customers agree with the statement, "If a brand understands me on a personal level, I'm more likely to be loyal to them."[47]

Case Study: charity: water

Just like in the corporate world, many important constituents exist in the non-profit world. One critical group, of course, is financial donors. The parallel to customer experience in the nonprofit sector is donor experience.

One major nonprofit with an incredible donor experience is called "charity: water," and its strategy provides potential lessons for businesses of all types.

The organization's mission is to provide fresh, clean drinking water to rural communities throughout the world that previously did not have access to it. Its founder, Scott Harrison, not only recognizes this as a critical health and economic crisis, he also set out to literally change how charities work.

At the core of his decision to redesign the charity structure was the fact that people generally don't trust charities. This was confirmed in research by *The Chronicle of Philanthropy* and reported by the Better Business Bureau. After surveying 2,100 adults in the United States, it found that "while the majority of respondents (73 percent) say it is very important to trust a charity before giving, only a small portion of respondents (19 percent) say they highly trust charities and an even smaller portion (10 percent) are optimistic about the sector becoming more trustworthy over time."[48]

A major aspect of trusting a charity is knowing where a donation is going; is it going to the main advertised cause, or is much of it being wasted in administrative costs?

To combat this inherent struggle, Harrison designed his organization in a novel way: by creating two companies. The first was the charity itself, which would build wells around the world to provide fresh water access to the poorest communities. To combat the trust issue, Harrison wanted to ensure (and be able to market) that 100 percent of all donations, big or small, would go toward well building.

So how did he cover the overhead expenses of such an ambitious operation? By ingeniously creating a second company and asking wealthy benefactors and celebrities to fund it. He even set up two bank accounts, one to cover operational expenses and the other to build the wells.

Knowing that the full amount of donations would go to well building was a good start, but Harrison didn't stop there.

The organization created dozens of real-life stories and videos showing families seeing fresh water for the first time, drinking and bathing in clean water for the first time, and experiencing the pure joy and appreciation that accompanies a new well installation. Regular emails detail success stories from around the world, along with statistics, interviews, and more storytelling. They give donors the feeling that the money they contributed is making a real difference.

Then Harrison partnered with Google Maps to display on an interactive map all of the wells that charity: water has built so that donors can track their locations and water output in real time. (It's also how the charity can identify any malfunctioning wells.)

According to the charity: water website, "We track every dollar you raise, and show the projects you helped fund with photos and GPS. We've consistently received the highest grades available for accountability and transparency."

The organization also came up with the idea of having people donate their birthdays to provide water. What started as a small idea blossomed into thousands of people participating, from five-year-olds to 105-year-olds, with some raising only a few dollars and others raising into the six figures. I donated on my forty-fifth birthday and raised nearly $1,800.

All told, charity: water has raised more than $300 million thanks to the generosity of more than a million people around the world. This has allowed them to bring clean drinking water to more than 29,000 villages serving more than 8.4 million people in twenty-eight countries.

So what does charity: water have to do with your business? Here are some takeaways:

- Listen to your potential customer base. Ask them what they like and don't like so you can build a business model that takes those thoughts and beliefs into consideration.

- Keep communicating with customers to let them know about their or your progress. If you are a B2B company, this could be about a project that you're working on together; for B2Cs, it's about making it easy to track the status of an order in real time.

- Be open and honest with your customers at all times to gain their trust. Customers appreciate communication that is about them and their needs, not just about the company and its needs.

If you do have a chance to support charity: water, I highly recommend it for the donor experience alone.

Case Study: Target

I had such a great experience buying and assembling a piece of furniture from Target that I wrote about it for *Forbes*.[49] Here is the story:

Anyone who has built a piece of furniture from that well-known Swedish company is familiar with the accompanying instruction guides, which contain pages and pages of directions with zero words. You just have to look at the pictures and hope they're self-explanatory.

Having not performed well in shop class in high school, I generally need more hand holding than just pictures. Enter Target, and its Threshold brand of do-it-yourself furniture.

I brought home the Low-Profile Media Stand and took everything out of the box. I was already sweating at the prospect of spending the next two hours of my life building this thing. I opened the instruction booklet expecting the worst, and was pleasantly surprised by the first paragraph (yes, there were actually words):

"Congratulations on your latest Target purchase. Now what? Don't start sweating over this box of parts. This will be easy. We did the hard work for you. All you need to do is follow our simple instructions and you'll be on your way to transforming your room in no time. Good luck, though we're confident you won't need it."

This is a bold promise, given that Target has no idea about my building talents (but they somehow knew about my sweating!)— especially my penchant for getting about three-quarters through before realizing I put some piece on backwards 12 steps prior.

But if they're confident that I won't need help or luck, then I'm confident. In the immortal words of Barney Stinson from How I Met Your Mother: *Challenge Accepted.*

So the first thing that Target did was completely change my attitude about the project, which was big because I'm not a guy who looks forward to building furniture. All it took was one paragraph of text to put me in a completely different mindset.

This is what we refer to on the Experience This! *podcast as "making the required remarkable." Build-it-yourself items have to come with instructions; that's the required part. Starting off with a paragraph that immediately gets your attention and puts you at ease is the remarkable part.*

The media stand instructions were only thirteen steps compared to what sometimes feels like fifty-seven steps with other products—definitely more manageable.

But Target also promised it would be "easy" because they "did the hard work" already. They were right. For example, the hinges on the cabinet doors—probably the most annoying part—came pre-installed. I can't tell you how many times I've tried to install those myself only to find that the cabinet door doesn't close correctly. So that step of putting the doors on was literally just snapping them into place. It was easy.

My son and I put the whole media stand together in less than a half an hour (I had budgeted two hours). We never ran into any trouble. All of the instructions had words as well as pictures, so it was super easy to follow. We both felt very accomplished when it was done.

This is a terrific example of taking something that could have been a lousy experience and turning it into something that was remarkable. And though Target's promise was indeed bold, the company successfully delivered on it. So the next time that I have to buy a piece of furniture that I'm going to need to build myself, where do you think I'll be shopping?

☆ ☆ ☆ ☆ ☆

Immersive doesn't have to be difficult or expensive to execute. But it does have to be thoughtful, intentional, and consistent. Companies must make a focused effort to understand their customers' needs and then exceed their expectations in a unique and memorable way.

Toward the beginning of my nearly ten-year career at Discover Card, I was struck by how often I saw the word "love" in customer feedback, as in: "I love my Discover Card." I couldn't help but wonder, *who loves a credit card?* I can understand loving brands like Starbucks or Disney or Apple, but a credit card?

It turns out that Discover's tireless dedication to the customer is what made people love their credit card. It wasn't just one thing, like the decision to invest in 100 percent US-based customer service, or to eliminate almost every fee, or to instruct customer service agents to stop trying to cross-sell and instead focus only on resolving each customer's issue. It was all of those things together.

When you are a truly customer-centric organization, and you take the time to really know and understand your customers and their journey with you, then being Immersive is the natural conclusion.

Chapter 7

SHAREABLE

Now that you've learned how to be Witty and create Immersive experiences, let's talk about being Shareable. Think of Shareable as creating the desire to tell someone else about the experience. Often we accomplish this via social media, but it can also mean telling friends, family, and colleagues in person, on the phone, or via email.

"Make your products shareable," advises messaging platform Podium. "This is one of the best marketing strategies because nothing is more personal than a friend recommending something to you."[50]

Shareable may seem like the most obvious of the WISE elements; after all, who doesn't want word-of-mouth marketing? Yet businesses create experiences every single day that customers aren't sharing.

According to marketing consultancy IMPACT, 75 percent of people do not believe brand advertising, but 92 percent believe brand recommendations from a friend. What's more, word-of-mouth marketing generates twice the sales as paid ads.[51] Yet most companies spend infinitely more of their marketing budget on paid advertising than on customer experience.

Remembering that the definition of customer experience includes every single interaction a customer has with a brand, we must consider how every experience looks when shared. This can range from digital imagery in an advertisement to almost any element of a physical experience.

Consider these two coffee mugs:

One is a plain white mug, situated next to a white notebook. The rustic wood table is kind of cool, but this photo is otherwise dull and unremarkable. The other mug has brightly colored stripes, and while it's sitting on a neutral-colored table, the bright green blurred background gives the viewer a sense of the outdoors, perhaps on a deck or patio.

Now there is nothing wrong with a white mug. It certainly doesn't affect the taste of the coffee. But would you rather share a picture of the plain white mug or the colorful striped one?

If you're not in the coffee business, remember that this is not about the coffee or the mug. It's about looking at every part of your experience and asking, "Is this worthy of sharing?"

Often, I remind audiences and clients that there's no such thing as an "offline" experience anymore. We used to have offline experiences: an airplane, a subway, an office meeting, a bedroom rendezvous. But now everything we do, everywhere we go, we can pull out our phones, take a picture or video, and turn an offline experience into an online experience.

So with every part of your company's experience, you have to ask yourself if you want it shared on social media. This is not just about being afraid of what people might say, it's about how you design it so people *want* to share the experience.

☆ ☆ ☆ ☆ ☆

It's getting harder and harder for marketers and salespeople to break through the clutter of the inbox. Consider how many emails a typical decision-maker at a Fortune 500 company gets each day; it's often in the hundreds. So if you want to stand out, you have to be different. One of the best ways to do that may seem old-fashioned, but it's effective: snail mail.

Americans are getting less mail at home, and most people don't get much mail at all in the office. So when they do get snail mail, they are more likely to open it. Imagine a near-100 percent open rate on an email campaign, and that's what you get with the good old Postal Service.

Enter Punkpost, a high-tech solution with a low-tech product. Punkpost has a small army of human artists who design, write, and mail handwritten greeting cards. Customers can use the website or mobile app to choose a card, create the text in less time than it takes to craft an entire email, and even add extras like photos and confetti. Then the Punkpost artists execute and send your masterpiece within twenty-four hours.

The cost is essentially the same as going to the store, buying a greeting card, putting a stamp on it, and mailing it. Recipients absolutely love the cards.

"Everyone knows that feeling of finding a handwritten note in your mailbox," said Punkpost cofounder and CEO Lex Monson. "It's something so simple, but it gives this big reaction from whoever gets it."[52]

Indeed, one thing that is different about a Punkpost card is that people are much more likely to keep it and display it because it's a work of art. Every time they look at it, or a colleague notices it, the sender is remembered.

"People do hang them up by their desk or on their refrigerator, and then every time they look at it, they're reminded of you and your awesome service," Monson said.

Do you think anybody did that the last time you sent them an email? Probably not.

Recipients also love sharing Punkpost cards on social media.

"People will legit post it on Facebook and Twitter," Monson said. "Especially for salespeople [for whom] a lot of their business comes from referrals, it's enormous for them to get that sort of thing."

Realtors love Punkpost, Monson said, because it allows them to celebrate the closing of a home and a "houseaversary" every year thereafter.

Monson noted that the surprise factor is what makes it so Shareable.

"Getting a card from a friend or family member is awesome and surprising, but then getting it from someone who you see more in a professional setting is extra, like, 'I did not expect this from them. This is so cool,'" she said.

This is such an easy and inexpensive way to create a Shareable moment. Think about it the next time you sign a big deal, accomplish a big project milestone, or just want to celebrate an occasion with a client.

☆ ☆ ☆ ☆ ☆

Sipsmith, a UK gin company, hosted a tasting at a festival in Chicago. Normally, at a spirits tasting at a grocery store or liquor store, the customer is handed a tiny plastic cup filled only with the high-propane liquid. But that's not how most people drink, so it's not as effective of a trial mechanism as it could be.

Sipsmith set up an entire bar at the festival, complete with a bartender dressed in branded clothing. The bartender welcomed the customer—me—and then asked what kind of tonic I would like with my gin. *What kind of . . . tonic?* I wondered. I was actually a bartender in my previous life, and I had no idea that different kinds of tonic exist.

So I learned all about a manufacturer called Fever-Tree and its Mediterranean tonic (made "by blending essential oils from the flowers, fruits and herbs" of the Mediterranean[53]), Indian tonic (made using "a handful of different botanicals, including our distinctive natural quinine and oils from Mexican Bitter Oranges"[54]), and citrus tonic. (Incidentally, Fever-Tree also offers Lemon, Cucumber, Pink Grapefruit, Aromatic, and Elderflower tonics.)

After choosing a tonic, the customer is motioned over to the Garnish Bar. Normally a gin and tonic just has a squeeze of lime; it's actually one of the most basic drinks at the bar. But at the Garnish Bar, lemons, cherries, dried strawberries, black pepper, rose petals, and more beckoned—all items I heretofore would never have imagined in a gin and tonic.

In fact, I did the math for you: If you combine the tonic choices and the garnish choices, over a *billion* possible combinations of cocktails exist! The experience doesn't end there.

After creating their drink, the customer walks to one last station where they get a little card and marker in order to name their own drink. Someone then hands them a tiny clothespin so they can clip the nametag to their drink for all to see.

What do you think happens next? Everyone takes a picture of their personalized drink and posts it on social media. Talk about an Instagram-worthy moment! Compared to the liquor store gulp, this is a fun and truly Shareable experience that brings a lot of new fans to the Sipsmith brand.

Note that Sipsmith combined Immersive and Shareable in its tasting experience, which is why it was so effective. Designing the drink is the Immersive part; naming it with a personalized sign is what makes it Shareable.

When I worked at Discover Card, the company ran a campaign where it sent out a $5 Starbucks gift card to all new cardmembers after their first ninety days. There was no ask. There was no sales pitch. It just said, "Discover loves to spoil our cardmembers. Enjoy a $5 treat on us."

At the time, I was leading the social media team, so we asked for, and received, permission to add just one more thing to the accompanying card: the #discoverjoy hashtag. This was in the early days of social media, and someone asked, "What if somebody doesn't know what to do with a hashtag?" The answer: "Don't worry about it, because that's not whom we're talking to anyway!"

What happened after those cards were mailed was absolutely incredible. People shared and shared and shared . . . and shared and shared and shared pictures of that $5 gift card thousands of times on social media. Then, a few days later, another wave of shares rippled through. But these were different; these were shares of the Starbucks drinks that cardmembers had bought with their gift card! Virtually every one of them thanked Discover for the drink.

These were $5 gift cards; they weren't life-changing. But the campaign was the right combination of true "surprise and delight" with no strings attached and a gentle nudge to share with friends and followers.

The technique may seem obvious years later, but if you look at all of the marketing that you send out (or get from other companies), the hashtag is rarely there anymore.

Speaking of Starbucks, the coffee giant created what was probably the most Shareable coffee beverage in history with the Unicorn Frappuccino. The drink was "made with a sweet dusting of pink powder, blended into a crème Frappuccino with mango syrup and layered with a pleasantly sour blue drizzle. It is finished with vanilla whipped cream and a sprinkle of sweet pink and sour blue powder topping."[55]

Why was the drink so Shareable? There were several reasons:

- It had limited availability; it was only available for five days in April 2017.
- It created a giant fear of missing out (or FOMO as the millennials call it).
- It was a beautiful product that was immediately Instagram-ready.
- Like Against the Grain's "Old Fashioned Experience," it evolved as the customer drank it. To wit: "Like its mythical namesake, the Unicorn Frappuccino blended crème comes with a bit of magic, starting as a purple beverage with swirls of blue and a first taste that is sweet and fruity. But give it a stir and its color changes to pink, and the flavor evolves to tangy and tart. The more swirl, the more the beverage's color and flavors transform."[56]

So not surprisingly, Starbucks had thousands and thousands of people talking about, and sharing pictures of, the Unicorn Frappuccino—until it was gone.

You might have noticed I wrote that the Unicorn Frappuccino was "the most Shareable *coffee* beverage in history." The "coffee" adjective was no accident, because the most Shareable beverage in history goes to . . . Coca-Cola for its iconic "Share a Coke" marketing campaign.

The soda giant began its historic campaign in Australia in 2011 and soon launched it in the United States with 250 of the most popular first names emblazoned on the sides of twenty-ounce bottles. Customers were encouraged to find their own names, find their friend's names, and, of course, share a Coke with someone IRL (in real life) or by using the hashtag #ShareaCoke on social media.

The social media reaction was stunning. According to *Investopedia*, consumers shared more than 500,000 photos via the #ShareaCoke hashtag within the campaign's first year alone. Coca-Cola also gained roughly 25 million new Facebook followers that same year.[57]

The campaign is also credited with reversing a decade-long decline in sales in the United States.[58]

Coca-Cola knew it had a hit on its hands, and it kept innovating to make the campaign consistently feel fresh.

In 2015, the company expanded to 1,000 names and offered custom-printed orders for people whose names still weren't included.[59] In Mexico, the company even started adding people's names to cans in Braille.[60] Then in 2018, Coke converted the name labels into removable stickers that could be more easily shared and also affixed to items such as phones or notebooks, making them even more Shareable.[61]

Some similarities exist between the success of the Unicorn Frappuccino and the Share a Coke campaign. The latter was largely successful because:

- 💡 It had limited availability.
- 💡 It created a game or challenge to find one's name or the name of a loved one.
- 💡 It was easily photographable.
- 💡 It was the first example of mass, nondigital personalization.
- 💡 It actually affected people's brains; scientists have found that "hearing one's own name has unique brain functioning activation specific to one's own name in relation to the names of others"—"including [in the] middle frontal cortex, middle and superior temporal cortex, and cuneus."[62]

Did you end up finding your name on a can or bottle? I did (though I had to make do with "Daniel"), and, of course, I shared it on all of my social media profiles.

☆ ☆ ☆ ☆ ☆

My teenage son has good (and expensive) taste in food, so he chose to celebrate his birthday at Fleming's Steakhouse. When I booked the reservation on OpenTable, a restaurant booking app, I noted that we were celebrating his birthday.

Most sit-down restaurants will bring out a (usually) complimentary dessert with a candle and have some of the staff sing "Happy Birthday" to the guest of honor. That's fun if only to embarrass the birthday boy or girl, but it's not necessarily Shareable because it's become so typical.

Fleming's Steakhouse made it clear that they weren't offering the "typical" experience when, immediately upon being seated at our table, the *maître d'* presented my son with an envelope containing a birthday card. The front of the card said "Happy Birthday" in script letters, and the inside stated in print: "Happy birthday to you. Thank you for celebrating with us. Best wishes from your friends at Fleming's Prime Steakhouse and Wine Bar." Someone then wrote "And many more!" in ink at the bottom.

Honestly, if that's all Fleming's had done, I would have been impressed, because they used the information they had at their disposal—the note I included with the reservation—and made my son feel special from the moment he sat down.

So many companies neglect to do this. Think about how many companies know your birthday because you've filled out a form or entered it online or had to show your driver's license. The DMV, airport security, the hotel check-in desk, bartenders and bouncers, any store selling alcohol or cigarettes, insurance brokers, mortgage brokers, bankers, and so many more—they all know our birthday.

Now think about how many of them have ever wished you a happy birthday.

The most fascinating time to test this theory is on your actual birthday; see how many times you can show your ID, and count the number of people who notice it's your big day. (Full disclosure: This happens to me more often than most since my birthday is on Christmas Day, December 25th!)

As we enjoyed our meal at Fleming's, we couldn't help but wonder what the "free dessert" would be, and after seeing the card, we suspected it might not be "typical."

Sure enough, the waiter brought out a beautiful box containing four hand-made chocolate truffles atop a plate with "Happy Birthday" and the Fleming's logo stenciled in cocoa powder, along with a sparkler instead of a candle (which, let's face it, is way more cool). Not surprisingly, everyone pulled out their phones to take a picture of the sparkling chocolates—the kids to share on Snapchat and Instagram Stories, and the adults to share on Facebook.

Again, the sparkler alone would have likely made this experience stand out compared to other birthday experiences, but it was the bookended combination of the greeting card and the special dessert that made it so memorable—and Shareable.

This story reminded me of another birthday experience, this time when I was a student at the University of Pennsylvania. At dinner with a bunch of friends, we learned that our waitress was working her last night at the restaurant. So we decided to have some fun with her. We told her that we were members of the Penn Birthday Club, which paired together people with the same birthdays and paid for them to go out to dinner.

"Wait, it's *all* of your birthdays?" she asked incredulously. We all kept a straight face and nodded yes. As poor college students, of course, our goal was to end up with free dessert for everyone.

The waitress remained skeptical. Every time she stopped by the table, she asked the same question in a different way: "Are you *sure* it's all of your birthdays?" "Are you really telling the truth?" "Are you guys pulling my leg?"

We kept the gag going for the entire dinner. Only after we were finished and she asked one last time did we finally admit that we were just playing with her.

A few moments later, she emerged with an entire cake filled with candles and had multiple staff members sing "Happy Birthday" to the entire table! Needless to say, her last night at the restaurant resulted in one of her largest tips ever. While I couldn't share that experience on social media back in the mid-1990s, I still share it with people today.

One last story about being Shareable comes from an unlikely source: a French art museum. The Musée d'Orsay, a museum in Paris, is housed in a railway station built in the late 1800s. It displays mainly French art dating from that same time period. It also houses the largest collection of Impressionist and Postimpressionist masterpieces in the world by painters including Monet, Manet, Degas, Renoir, Cezanne, Seurat, and van Gogh.[63]

In January 2020, the museum announced that painter, illustrator, and writer Jean-Philippe Delhomme (of *New Yorker* and *GQ* cartoon fame) was its first "Instagram artist in residence."[64]

Each week, Delhomme creates and shares an Instagram post from a famous artist or cultural figure that looks like it could be real but actually originates from a fictitious Instagram account (good thing, since most of these figures are long dead). Other historical figures chime in from their faux accounts as well.

The project has served to introduce old French art to a new audience and is a really interesting way to connect with younger, future potential patrons and get them interested in visiting the museum. We have more access to educational content than ever before in the history of humankind, so it makes sense that a museum, which is an educational institution, is taking advantage of that. In this case, a museum in Paris can expand its reach globally and make an impact.

It also speaks to how a lot of older institutions mistakenly believe that everybody knows about art or whatever it is that is featured in the museum because the employees and docents live and breathe it every day. The same is true for employees of corporations; you may be involved every day in widgets and know everything about widgets, but that doesn't mean that your customer or your prospective customer has the same love for widgets or the same knowledge.

For businesses that are afraid of social media or don't think they're cool enough to be on the "Insta," the Musée d'Orsay demonstrates that anyone and anything can be new again and can be Shareable if you're willing to experiment and try something different.

By the way, the museum's Instagram account boasts more than a million followers.

Chapter 8

EXTRAORDINARY

W e've talked about being Witty, especially with language, and how that is different from trying to be hilarious. We discussed being Immersive so our customers can feel the experience in their bones and remember all of it. We've learned what makes experiences Shareable to friends, family, and social media followers. So now we've come to the "E" in WISE. It stands for "Extraordinary."

Sometimes Extraordinary is where I start to lose people because they think, *I can't afford Extraordinary; it's too expensive.* Yes, I could share tons of customer experience examples with you right now where companies spent millions of dollars to create unbelievable experiences.

We could talk about the high-end hotel that built a dock overnight for a wheelchair-bound guest so she and her husband could dine at the high-end "floating restaurant."

There's the story of Ally Bank celebrating "Banksgiving" by having its agents finish calls with "Is there anything else I can help you with today?" and then giving the customer literally whatever they asked for next. This wound up ranging from a $25 gift card to a fall yard cleanup to a holiday visit to see family to a $55,000 grant toward a good cause.[65]

Or of course we could reminisce about Oprah giving away a car to everyone in her studio audience.

These are all fantastic stories, but I'm not sharing any of them in detail because they don't have the three qualities I look for when designing remarkable experiences: being simple, practical, and inexpensive.

So don't worry. You don't need a ton of money to be Extraordinary.

Extraordinary really just means "better than ordinary." Your experience is probably ordinary right now, which is why people aren't sharing things about your brand. But the good news is that the bar for customer experience is exceedingly low. You only have to get a little bit over it to be better than ordinary and have people take notice.

Remember when we talked earlier about how so many experiences are *meh* and no one shares a so-so experience? All we have to do is be a little bit better than *meh* and we're going to find ourselves in that positive experience area that people want to talk about with friends and family.

☆ ☆ ☆ ☆ ☆

If you're like me and travel a lot for work, that means you also stay in a lot of hotels. There's a dirty little secret about frequent travelers that most of us don't want to admit: Sometimes we wake up in the middle of the night with absolutely no idea where we are.

"Am I in my bedroom? No, it's a hotel, but wait . . . which hotel is it again? Where is the bathroom? And why is it so dark?"

Even if you don't travel frequently, waking up at night in a strange place can be quite disorienting.

At one hotel I stayed at (naturally, I can't remember which one), I woke up in the middle of the night to go to the bathroom. As soon as my feet hit the floor, a motion-activated light turned on from the bottom of the nightstand. *It lit the path to the bathroom!* Brilliant.

Now, being the customer experience guy that I am and needing this picture, I got down on my hands and knees and examined the light. It surprised me to find that it was a small stick-on light that probably costs fifty cents at Home Depot. Clearly it was not

expensive, but it completely changed the experience of getting up in the middle of the night in a dark hotel. That counts as Extraordinary in my book. (Literally.)

☆ ☆ ☆ ☆ ☆

In my first book, *Winning at Social Customer Care: How Top Brands Create Engaging Experiences on Social Media*, I highlighted an example of a conference call company's on hold experience. It remains one of my favorite stories to tell, especially with the addition of an audio snippet to my keynote speeches, so I just had to share it again in this book because it is so remarkable.

On a typical conference calling system, when you dial in before the host you have to wait on hold while listening to absolutely horrible elevator music. The folks at UberConference wanted to do something different and create a unique experience at an unexpected time.

While waiting on hold on the UberConference system, you hear a guy strumming on his guitar and singing lyrics about waiting on hold for a conference call to start.

The song is called "I'm On Hold," and the artist is Alex Cornell. You can hear the entire song on YouTube.[66] It is definitely worth a listen.

Cornell and UberConference took an ordinary, unremarkable experience—waiting on hold—and made it Extraordinary. The improvement is so powerful that I found myself hoping the other party would wait to join the conference call until the song was over!

☆ ☆ ☆ ☆ ☆

A restaurant in Chicago called Osteria via Stato, and owned by the ubiquitous Lettuce Entertain You group, is separated into two sections by a set of swinging doors. A constant stream of people flowed through these doors the day I visited—customers, waiters with big trays of food, busboys with water pitchers, etc.—and I wondered how nobody was crashing into one another. How was that possible in such a busy restaurant?

So being the customer experience guy that I am, I took a closer look.

In the United States, usually two words appear on any retail or restaurant doors. No, I'm not thinking of "In" and "Out" or "Enter" and "Exit." I'm thinking of "Push" and "Pull," two English words, both four letters long, and both starting with "p-u."

But people confuse "Push" and "Pull" all the time; we've all seen it. Maybe you do too, and maybe you remember pulling and pulling on a door that wouldn't open, only to realize the sign said "Push."

Osteria via Stato avoided this problem entirely by using perhaps the two easiest English words—"Yes" and "No." And you know what? Not one person got it wrong. That's a good result when you're talking about employee and customer safety plus not wanting people's meals to end up on the floor.

Was this an easy change? Yes. Did it cost anything? Not that I know of. Yet it's Extraordinary because it effectively solves a real potential problem and does so with a little "wink-wink" to anyone who notices.

Marketo is a marketing automation software company. Like many SaaS (software-as-a-service) companies, Marketo offers downloadable resources in exchange for supplying an email address. Typically, these are white papers or ebooks boasting of "thought leadership" and full of charts and graphs and maybe a proprietary survey.

One particular resource caught my eye on Marketo's website: *The Definitive Guide to Lead Generation Workbook.* As an entrepreneur searching for speaking and coaching opportunities, I'm always interested to learn new lead generation techniques.

What I didn't expect in the workbook, and what made it Extraordinary (remember: just better than ordinary) was a color-by-number picture of two buyer "personas" and a word search puzzle filled with marketing jargon.

It didn't cost Marketo anything to add these elements, but they made it fun and they made it different from every single other white paper or e-book that I have downloaded.

Case Study: Savannah Bananas

The Savannah Bananas are an independent baseball team in a summer college league—a level or two below in quality of an "A-level" Minor League Baseball team. The owner, Jesse Cole, admitted that the Bananas are "an average baseball team" in an interview for this book.[67]

So how in the world does the team sell out every single game and have a ticket-waiting list that is thousands of fans long?

It's because of Cole's relentless focus on the fan experience, a strategy he calls "Fans First."

"We have a Fans First playbook that every single person on our staff goes through," Cole said. "A player can't put on a uniform until they go through our Fans First U. onboarding. An intern goes through it; a game day staff member goes through it. We spend so much time on teaching Fans First because that's who we are."

Being a big baseball fan myself, I asked him what exactly is wrong with baseball as it is.

"It's too long. It's too slow. It's too boring," he said. "You get nickeled-and-dimed. It's about corporate money . . . [When] you watch a baseball game, look at the people behind home plate. Very few people are actually watching the game. They're on their phones. They're talking to people. That's a problem."

"Then the next problem," he continued, "is they leave the game in the middle of the game. When was the last time someone came to a great movie and was like, 'Oh, it was a great movie. I left in the middle.' It doesn't happen. Yet [in] baseball it happens every single night. So there's fundamental problems and unfortunately, baseball is not doing anything about it."

Cole's answer as to *why* baseball isn't doing anything about it is simple: money.

"The challenge is if you have tremendous success and you're making billions of dollars, which Major League Baseball is, why would you change? They're making more money every single year; every single year the TV rights [are] getting bigger, the sponsorship deals are getting bigger, but their attendance is declining dramatically. Why would the owners fundamentally change their model to be more about their fans?"

Sure enough, Major League Baseball generated about $9.9 billion in total revenue in 2018, which was twice the revenue generated ten years before, according to Statista.[68] And total attendance has fallen every season since 2012, according to Baseball Reference.[69]

Here is just a sampling of the sights you might take in at a Savannah Bananas baseball game:

- A ticket employee who delivers thank you calls as a rap
- A break-dancing first base coach
- A senior citizen dance team
- A male cheerleading team
- A professional wrestler as the trainer/intimidation coach
- A grandma coach
- Ticket takers in banana costumes punching banana-shaped tickets
- A "Professional High-Fiver"

- Players performing choreographed dances
- "Dolce and Banana" underwear
- Players going on dates with fans in the middle of the game
- Cole himself walking the stands in his trademark yellow tuxedo

And to answer the nickel-and-diming complaint of typical baseball games, every ticket is all-inclusive so fans can eat and drink whatever they want.

In fact, more than 150 promotions, skits, games, songs, and dances might be performed during a game. And while there are a few regular bits, every game day experience is intentionally different.

One thing that makes the Bananas' success so remarkable is Cole's willingness to try almost anything.

"There was zero strategy in the beginning; it was mostly just test and experiment," he said. "So the first step, we said, 'All right, what can change the perception? What can we be the only one doing?'"

That question led to the choreographed dancing idea, where Cole brought in a local dance instructor to teach the players how to dance.

The result?

"Fans started going nuts; they wanted autographs," Cole said. "I remember going through the crowd and a woman put her arm over on her husband and said, 'Shut up, honey, they're about to dance.' It was like, 'We got something.'"

So Cole doubled down on entertainment—the crazier, the better.

"What are the most unique things we can do to get people to leave and say, 'You wouldn't believe what happened at the ballpark tonight,'" he said. "And that's not a baseball game. Everyone has seen a home run. Everyone has seen a strike-out. So you need something people haven't seen, and you can't rely on the sport because the sport is a hundred years old."

"We can't be the best in baseball," he added. "We *can* be the best at the entertaining, [with] baseball as our stage."

Many ideas emerge from a concept Cole dubs "Ideapaloozas," which are held monthly to encourage employees to come up with the next great entertainment idea and answer the perpetual question of "What's next?"

"I think so many people are so scared to test things because they're afraid of losing, they're afraid of what people are going to think," Cole said. "But when you build your brand on doing fun, unique, different things, they give you the benefit of the doubt."

The Fans First mantra permeates the entire organization.

"We all have one job; everyone's job is to entertain our fans—that's it," Cole said. "There's no difference between a player or a front office member, a game day staff member, or an owner, or president . . . Everyone knows when the gates open up, we're always on stage. Every game is someone's first game, and so that's the mindset no matter what your 'level' on the team."

Does all the goofiness end up offending the sensibilities of an actual baseball fan?

"One thousand percent," Cole said. "Of course it insults and upsets traditional baseball fans, and we've lost some of them, but that's not who we're targeting."

Cole recalls losing some season ticket holders early on who said, "It's just too much of a circus." Cole's response: "Perfect. Tell everyone that."

"Our target audience is anyone who really wants to have fun, not take themselves too seriously, and aren't stuck on the old ways of doing things, which is a much bigger opportunity than the people that are the traditionalists," he said.

How well do Cole and the Bananas appeal (a-*peel*?) to the target audience?

"When we did things like everyone else, we sold two total season tickets in our first three months . . . Even Little League teams didn't want to go to our games," Cole said. "Now, because of the experience, we have a priority waitlist up to 5,000 and every single game is sold out." (The team's road games typically have only a few hundred fans, something Cole says is "depressing.")

So what advice does Cole have for other businesses?

"You need something that people can actually talk about," he said. "You need something that's shareable, that's remarkable. We wanted people to say this wasn't like a typical baseball game, so they would spread the idea."

☆ ☆ ☆ ☆ ☆

In *Winning at Social Customer Care*, I shared the example of Malaysian video streaming service iflix and its corporate email disclaimer.

Instead of the standard "If you are the unintended recipient of this email, you must immediately destroy it or else . . .," the disclaimers at the bottom of iflix's corporate emails begin with "COVERING OUR BUTTS."[70]

Not surprisingly, people are drawn to the disclaimer and they actually read it—which is exactly what the lawyers want. In the case of iflix, the entire disclosure is worth reading because it's hilarious; it certainly could have fit in the Witty chapter.

Here is the full text of the email disclaimer:

> *COVERING OUR BUTTS: We know this email message and any accompanying attachments are full of fun and intriguing stuff, but they may contain information that is confidential and is subject to legal privilege. In other words, we could tell you, but then we'd have to kill you. Just kidding. There are other ways: If you are not the intended recipient, do not read, use, disseminate (it means "spread"), distribute or copy this message or attachments. If you have received this message in error (oops, our bad), please notify the sender immediately and delete the message. Any views, or bad jokes, expressed in this message, are those of the individual sender, except where the individual sender expressly states them to be the views of iflix (even the bad jokes). Before opening any attachments, please check them for viruses, defects and prepare to be amazed by the iflix revolution.*

Travel insurance provider Squaremouth took policy documentation to another level, thereby qualifying it for Extraordinary status.

"In an effort to highlight the importance of reading policy documents, we launched Pays to Read, a contest that rewards a $10,000 grand prize to the first individual to read their policy information from start to finish," the Squaremouth website reads.[71]

Donelan Andrews, a Georgia teacher and "self-proclaimed nerd" who "always reads the fine print,"[72] won the contest and the cash prize. Ironically, she often hid questions in her students' exams.

Why did Squaremouth go to the trouble of hiding a $10,000 price in an insurance policy?

"Over the past 16 years, we've learned that many travelers buy travel insurance and just assume they're covered if anything goes wrong, without actually reading the details of their policy. However, this often leads to claims for losses that are not covered. This lack of understanding is one of the biggest reasons travel insurance claims are denied."[73]

Denied insurance claims are some of the worst possible customer experiences, so Squaremouth is doing everything it can to educate consumers and prevent future disappointment. In the process, they had some fun and got some great media coverage from the contest, proving once again that when marketing and legal work together, great things can happen.

Remember that disclosures and fine print aim to explain the details to a customer. Often, people ask me how to deal with government regulation as a marketer because I've worked in both financial services and in healthcare, which are highly regulated.

I find that regulators generally have a good customer experience sense in mind when they create the regulations. If we start with the fact that the regulators, the lawyers, and the marketers all want customers to understand what they're getting themselves into, then we all should have the same goal of making sure that legal disclosures are easy to understand.

The problem arises when regulators tell companies exactly what to write, and that is generally not very customer friendly. Examples include radio commercials where the voiceover reads the disclosures so fast that you can hardly understand them, or pharmaceutical commercials on television that can't say what the product is actually for but always show a happy couple strolling on the beach and then list a dozen possible side effects of the drug.

Often, well-intentioned legislation mandates so much of the solution that marketers and customer experience professionals are left without much leeway for innovation.

Obviously, it shouldn't take $10,000 to get people to read your legal disclosures. Take the extra time to read them yourself. If you find that you are nodding off or drooling on the table, that means your customers are doing the same thing.

☆ ☆ ☆ ☆ ☆

Motorola Solutions is a telecommunications equipment provider that largely sells to other businesses and municipal or government units like public safety (it is no longer related to the smartphone manufacturer). Its products aren't sexy, but they are critical and often life-saving.

B2B marketers often believe they can't market like B2C companies because their products or services don't lend themselves as much to advertising. Motorola Solutions proved this theory wrong with a fantastic video that didn't feature its products so much as it featured the outcomes that its products provide.

The video,[74] set to music with no voiceover, shows police officers, firefighters, teachers, and medical professionals using Motorola Solutions equipment in their daily jobs and achieving Extraordinary results. Words appear on the screen for the viewer to read:

> *On any given day, every moment matters to someone somewhere.*
> *Every moment millions of people around the world are impacted by what we do.*
> *A policeman watches an intersection in Santiago, Chile.*
> *A surgeon reads a chart in Hangzhou, China.*
> *A hospital manages blood transfusions efficiently in Lyon, France.*
> *An engineer checks a flood gauge in Zaragoza, Spain.*
> *A family asks directions in Veracruz, Mexico.*
> *A shopper pays for a skirt in London, UK.*
> *A patient is rushed through a hospital in Victoria, Australia.*
> *A teacher grades exams in Davenport, Iowa, USA.*
> *Multiple fire crews coordinate their five-alarm response in Akita, Japan.*
> *Our innovations, products and solutions play essential roles in people's lives.*
> *Everywhere, every day.*
> *Right now we are saving seconds that can save his life.*
> *Keeping him in control of the chaos.*
> *Delivering critical data to the scene.*
> *Helping them learn and grow.*

Making just-in-time supply a reality.
Moving retailers closer to customers.
Connecting people around the world
Growing. Protecting. Empowering. Transforming.
We help people be their best in the moments that matter.
This is why we're here and why we do what we do.
This is our purpose.
This is our moment.
We are Motorola Solutions.

The video is Extraordinary because it isn't just a moving catalog of products; in fact, there isn't a single product mentioned in the entire ad. But it shows the impact of Motorola Solutions products in an emotional and evocative way. That's hard to do in the B2B world, but certainly not impossible.

Case Study: Chewy.com

Of all the brands I mention in my keynote speeches and blogs, Chewy.com, an online pet supplies company, most often elicits a response from at least one person in the audience which is akin to, "Let me tell you about my Chewy experience."

It is one of those universally loved brands that always puts customers first, and so it has created an army of raving fans.

Chewy strives to create remarkable experiences for its customers—the human ones and the furry ones. A website statement about the company's culture is clear on this point:

"At Chewy, we strive to deliver the best products with the best service—and we want to become even better. Happy customers are always our #1 priority, and our team members are passionate about finding new ways to wow both pet owners and the industry at large."[75]

When my high school friend Mike lost his cat of seventeen years, Homey, he called Chewy to cancel his regular delivery of Homey's doctor-prescribed food. He spoke with an agent named Diane.

"I'm sure she could tell I was taking it hard," Mike said. "I wasn't ready for him to go and besides processing my request, she took a few extra moments to offer condolences and talk to me about him. I remember thinking when I got off the phone that she cared and I really appreciated that."[76]

The story could have ended there, especially because Mike was ending his business relationship with Chewy. But instead of sending him to the dreaded retention department, Chewy chose to create a remarkable experience for a departing customer.

"A couple of days later, my wife and I were touched and surprised to receive a beautiful bouquet of flowers in a vase with a handwritten note offering more condolences from Diane and the Chewy team," Mike said. "It was a really nice gesture that won't be forgotten."

So what did Mike do? He shared his Chewy story on Facebook.

"It compelled me to share my story and pictures of the flowers on social media," Mike said. "That good karma grows and spreads. Their emphasis on building their customer relationships beyond just processing transactions—especially one like mine that would seem to be a last transaction—ultimately built a stronger bond between me and their company.

"I think it develops a loyal customer base and spreads the word better than any advertising campaign can," he added. "I wish more companies took Chewy.com's approach."

The key here? Chewy recognized this was an emotional time for Mike and his family, and they treated him with kindness and respect.

The company carefully inserted itself into the emotional situation not by acting as a marketer but as a friend. They recognized that even though Mike might not be a lifelong customer, he was deserving of a lifelong experience, one that he'll remember forever and tell others about because it's both profound and meaningful.

When Mike eventually adopted a new cat, guess which pet supplies company became his go-to resource?

Another customer, Mariangel, regularly orders food and litter for her cat from Chewy. Mariangel emailed Chewy after one of her regular shipments did not arrive as scheduled.

"They emailed me back so quickly, and they said, 'We're going to send you another box with everything free of charge. If you happen to get the first box, you can just keep it. It's fine. You keep it for free,'" Mariangel explained.[77]

The next day, she actually received both boxes because one was simply late and the replacement box was sent via overnight express shipping.

But Chewy wasn't done. A week after the missing box incident, Mariangel received a postcard that said, "Greetings from Florida from your friends at Chewy. com," and on the back a handwritten note said, "Hi, Mariangel. Welcome to Chewy. I hope your furry baby loves the cat toy. Paws and kisses, Jenny."

"I love the fact that it's handwritten and they actually paid attention to the toy that was delivered in my first box with them," Mariangel said. "The fact they're sending this is amazing. I just have it on my fridge, and I tell everyone that my cat has received mail from Chewy, which is great."

How can other companies take a page out of Chewy's customer experience playbook?

Be ready to respond to your customers during emotional or difficult times. Even if a customer is leaving, do your best to end the relationship on a positive note and in a meaningful way.

Connecting with someone about their pet is a powerful relationship builder—a fast track to their heart. When companies create emotional connections with customers, they strengthen the relationship by reminding their customers that they are dealing with human beings on the other end, not just a monolithic corporation. By the way, no matter what business you're in, you can ask about your customers' pets!

Going above and beyond, whether with a handwritten note or an unexpected "surprise and delight" moment, is one of the best ways to get your customers to sing your praises—not only to their friends and family but to the rest of the world on social media. This free word-of-mouth marketing is especially powerful in social media.

Every interaction a customer has with a brand is a customer experience opportunity. Unfortunately, many of these opportunities are missed or ignored, leaving customers to wonder whether the company with which they've chosen to do business really cares about them.

Months later, Mariangel left a negative review on Chewy's site for a certain brand of kitty litter. It wasn't a complaint about Chewy. It was about a specific product.

"I recently switched litter for my cat and the one I selected was awful—even though it has great reviews. It just didn't work for us," Mariangel said in a direct message on Twitter. "I left a negative review—but not hating Chewy, or the brand, but more stating that it didn't work for long-haired cats."[78]

She added that she wasn't expecting anything, but she just wanted to warn other long-haired cat owners.

Shortly thereafter, she received an unexpected email from Chewy. To fully appreciate the brilliance of this customer service email, it is helpful to break it down into three parts:

The beginning: solving the problem. The email began: "Hi Mariangel. Your review on the [brand removed] wood clumping cat litter made me want to get in touch with you. I'm sorry to hear that the litter didn't quite work out. As pet parents, we always want to do right by our fuzzy families and get them everything they love, but sometimes swinging and missing happens. Anytime an item doesn't work out, please don't hesitate to let us know. We'll always make it right. In the meantime, I've processed a refund of $16.14 to the card used in the purchase and that should reflect back in your bank account in three to five days. Feel free to donate whatever you have left of the box to a rescue, or local shelter, or give that to a friend in need."

This email is remarkable because it is unexpected, friendly, and empathetic, and the customer gets a refund with no questions asked. She didn't even have to ask for the refund nor did she have to ship back the heavy litter to the company. It was a nice touch to suggest some options for what Mariangel could do with the leftover litter.

The middle: going above and beyond. The email continues: "I wanted to help further by finding some other litters that may help you. I did some digging and even found that [brand removed] has a variety made specifically for long-haired cats. Here are my suggestions." The email then lists four suggestions from four brands of cat litter that are appropriate for long-haired cats.

This part of the email is notable because the customer service agent isn't just solving the problem of the refund but taking the extra step to help Mariangel solve what might be the bigger problem: that she doesn't have litter that works for her cat. This wasn't necessary or expected, but it's a great example of going above and beyond in customer service at little to no cost to the company.

The big finish: connecting with the customer. The email concludes with, "I hope this helps. Please give our love to Roma. Should you like to share any photos of [her], we have a spot on our furry wall of fame here at the office which would look purr-fect with [her] in it. For now, if you have any questions, or if there's anything we can do, don't hesitate to give us a meow at any time, day or night. We're always here for you."

The email ends by referencing Mariangel's cat by name, which establishes a personal connection, and then encouraging her to stay engaged with the brand by offering her cat a spot on the company's furry wall of fame. The concluding sentence, "We're always here for you," sounds more like an intimate friend than a pet supplies company.

This email may have taken a little extra time to write because it's lengthy and required a bit of research, but it hit all the key points of a great customer service interaction: It was friendly, conversational, genuinely helpful, and it went above and beyond.

It's no wonder that Chewy.com benefits from so much word-of-mouth marketing by its raving fans.

It is important to note, though, that this sort of email is replicable. In fact, I would bet that a lot of it is a template (fill in customer name, product name, refund amount, pet's name, etc.). But it certainly doesn't come off that way to the customer because it is so personalized.

Why is service so important for Chewy?

"A lot of people believe that customer service is the most important aspect of the experience. It is for some companies, [which] thrive because of their customer service," said Mary Drumond, chief marketing officer at Worthix, a self-adaptive survey platform that uses AI to understand customer decisions. "So for brands like Chewy, service is really, really important, especially because they're not competing based on price. They're actually even a little bit more expensive than some of their competitors. And quality also isn't really a thing because they're selling the same dog food that everybody else is selling. So what makes Chewy worth it to their customers? Well, we like to believe that it is special treatment, or they go above and beyond not only for their customers, but for the pets that consume their products."[79]

So how did Mariangel react to the email?

"I just received this email from them and I'm ecstatic," she said on Twitter. "I never asked for a refund. I was actually going to use the whole thing just because I don't want to throw anything out."[80]

The key takeaway? Chewy.com successfully turned a disappointed customer into an even more loyal one, just by taking a little extra time in its communication.

The company wasn't afraid of a complaint and didn't look to hide it. Instead, it embraced the opportunity to surprise and delight a loyal customer whose expectations were not met, thereby retaining an important customer.

Though this particular transaction didn't work out quite as expected, Mariangel knows exactly where she will buy her next bag of kitty litter.

☆ ☆ ☆ ☆ ☆

Amazon and Redefining Extraordinary

I recently picked out a set of pots and pans at a great price on Amazon Prime Day. When it arrived, I opened the box with excitement; but that excitement quickly turned to disappointment when I noticed that one of the glass lids was completely shattered.

I wanted to call the manufacturer to order a replacement lid, but I didn't see a brand name, address, or website anywhere on the box. So I called Amazon.

Interestingly, the woman who answered the phone did not know how to get in touch with the manufacturer either. But she had a better idea.

"You know what? I'm going to refund your purchase in its entirety," she said. "And why don't you just keep the pots and pans?"

In less than a minute, the Amazon Customer Service agent completely changed my outlook about the situation; she made my problem go away entirely because, all of a sudden, I didn't really care that I was missing a lid because I got free pots and pans!

This situation wasn't Amazon's fault, but they made it their problem, and then they solved the problem. That is the hallmark of a truly customer-centric company. When you go above and beyond to solve a customer's problem, they will love you even more—despite the fact that something went wrong.

Amazon has notoriously shunned short-term revenue for long-term profit, focusing on lifetime customer value instead of today's single transaction. And they give customers the benefit of the doubt, which, let's face it, the vast majority of them deserve.

Remember: Without customers, we don't have a business.

This is why I believe that Amazon is the greatest company on the planet. You may not like Amazon because you think it put beloved chains like Toys "R" Us, Radio Shack, and countless others out of business. Or you may hate Amazon because you think it destroyed your local businesses.

I've got news for you: Those beloved chains and local businesses destroyed themselves.

Toys "R" Us went out of business because it refused to adapt to today's customer. The store looked the same at the bitter end as it did when I was a child.

And Toys "R" Us had one major advantage over Amazon: physical locations. It should have been kids' and parents' go-to entertainment venue. It should have been the place where kids could try out any new toy before buying it, like the Lego Store. Instead, it was just rows and rows of retail products on shelves.

Cat & Mouse Games, a local toy store in the West Loop neighborhood of Chicago, understands its role as a local business.

The employees are trained like Amazon's recommendation engine; you tell them a board game you like, and they give you four more that you should try.

The most distinctive feature of this store, though, is in the back: a board game library. Shoppers can check out a game, sit down with a friend at a table, and try out the game before purchasing it. The store even hosts weekly game nights for singles.

As lovers of strategy games know, they can get quite expensive; some are priced upwards of $50 or even $70. Trying a game out before buying it provides exceptional value, so much so that customers are willing to pay a couple of dollars more at the local store for the game rather than buy it on Amazon.

Alas, Amazon is among the most talked and written about companies in the world, and for good reason. The e-commerce giant has literally reinvented multiple industries, including bookstores and virtually every other retail category, third-party selling, subscription services, on-demand music and video, independent publishing, package delivery, voice assistants, cloud services, and many more.

Remarkably, throughout Amazon's growth story, it has never lost sight of its customers, repeatedly developing seamless user experiences and continuing to add value to its flagship Prime program.

Amazon has six Customer Service Tenets—posted throughout its offices and contact centers—which explain a lot about why the company is so easy and pleasurable to do business with. They can also be used as inspiration for any company looking to improve its customer service.

The six tenets are:

1. **"Relentlessly advocate for customers."** This is a truly amazing sentence because it demonstrates that Amazon clearly understands what many companies do not: Customers are not the enemy; they are the very reason a company exists. To "advocate" means to be on one's side, and the fact that Amazon "relentlessly" tries to be on the customer's side is indicative of why so many people love the company. In fact, by relentlessly advocating for its customers, Amazon has inspired millions of customers to advocate for Amazon!

2. **"Trust our customers and rely on associates to use good judgment."** When you trust your customers, they trust you back. Yes, a small minority of customers will try to take advantage of this trust, but most will not. In this tenet, what's also implied but not explicitly stated is that Amazon trusts its associates too. By giving them the freedom to "use good judgment," the company frees its associates from rigid scripts and empowers them to help solve customer problems. Since happy employees equal happy customers, the effect of this trust is felt beyond just the individual associate.

3. **"Anticipate customer needs and treat their time and attention as sacred."** This tenet can be broken down into two pieces. Anticipating customer needs in customer service means taking an educated guess about why someone is calling—a question about when a recent order will be delivered, for example—or even solving problems before a customer calls. For example, Amazon has been known to proactively issue refunds for video purchases if it notices that they downloaded too slowly.

   Too many companies act like they don't treat a customer's "time and attention as sacred." Examples include long hold times on the telephone or in a checkout line, not answering emails or social media posts, and forcing customers to jump through all sorts of hoops to make a claim, get a refund, or cancel an account. But Amazon knows that treating customers well and valuing their time will gain even more advocacy from raving fans.

4. **"Deliver personalized, peculiar experiences that customers love."** Did that word "peculiar" surprise you too? Everyone is trying to be "personalized" these days, but Amazon has proven time and time again that it is not "everyone." By being just a little bit peculiar—try asking Alexa to "beat box," for example—Amazon and its products become so much more memorable to customers. You might have also noticed the word "love" and might be thinking that no one could "love" your business. That's what I thought when I started working at Discover Card until I saw countless pieces of cardmember feedback using that very word. If someone can "love" their credit card, then someone can probably love your business too.

5. **"Make it simple to detect and systematically escalate problems."** This one is more operational in nature but still contains several key words: making it "simple" means making the customer service agent's job easier, and it connects back to valuing a customer's time. Being able to easily "escalate" problems to a supervisor or management is critical to early identification of potential outages or major public relations issues and connects back to trusting its associates to escalate when necessary. Doing so "systematically" means that Amazon is practicing continuous improvement so that it is constantly identifying and fixing issues to improve the overall customer experience.

6. **"Eliminate customer effort through this sequential and systematic approach: defect elimination, self-service, automation, and support from an expert associate."** Amazon doesn't just want to reduce customer effort. It wants to "eliminate" it! This is the real reason why Amazon is winning in so many different industries: It creates an effortless experience for its customers. The "sequential and systematic approach" makes so much sense: The fewer problems exist, and the more customers can solve those problems themselves (or have them automatically solved for them), the less the company is going to spend on traditional customer service. Amazon even spells out the order in which associates should attempt to reduce customer effort.

Many people lament Amazon's success because of its impact on local businesses. But if those local businesses had a set of Customer Service Tenets like Amazon's, they'd be far less likely to lose customers just because a product is a few dollars cheaper online.

Amazon is so great at what it does because it focuses on the customer experience at every touchpoint, fixes problems immediately and permanently, empowers its associates to do the right thing, and continuously improves on itself.

After the pots and pans experience mentioned earlier, I asked my Facebook friends to share the last remarkable experience they had with a brand. Interestingly, many of those experiences started out with a problem as well.

Sandy responded by saying that Bombas sent seven pairs of socks instead of the eight that she ordered. "The customer service department was swamped, and they were unable to respond within the timeframe promised. They not only refunded my entire purchase amount but issued me a $50 gift card for a future purchase."

Jamie singled out OtterBox: "They will provide you with a new phone case if yours gets stretched out or cracked. No questions asked."

Katie replied: "Glossier had apparently discovered an issue with the pigment changing in some makeup that I bought. I had not noticed any issues. They both refunded my money and sent me a new bottle once they'd fixed the issue."

Margaret shared that Wegmans called her house to tell her that a bag of flour she bought weeks ago had been recalled. (That one stunned me by the way.)

Dan wrote, "I was processing payroll while our HR manager was on vacation. A unique situation came up, so I called ADP for help. The person quickly understood what was needed, entered it into our payroll system so I didn't have to do it and potentially screw it up, and double-checked the information. It was a lifesaver, and I didn't have to bother my HR manager on her vacation."

Stacy shared that All-Clad replaced two of her ten-year-old nonstick pans because they'd lost their nonstick coating. She received two brand-new pans with no questions asked.

Lisa mentioned a car dealer who sent a driver with her mom's car to swap out the loaner car because "he knows how tough it is for me to get an additional aide to stay with my mom when there are car issues."

Jeffery posted: "I was at Whole Foods in the checkout line. An item I had from the Butcher Block, 1.5 pounds of pork chops, wasn't scanning out correctly because the barcode was faded. The cashier called them and told them to change out the toner on the scale. He proceeded to place the pork chops in my bag. I asked him how much, and he said they're free today because of the inconvenience of waiting for them to change out the toner. When in our lifetimes can we actually cry out free pork chops, and have it ring true?"

Julia said, "Bentley's Pet Store called me within twenty-four hours letting me know they overcharged me for my purchase by 50 percent and offered a credit. I would have never known. Love them."

Another Lisa shared, "I emailed Zappos to let them know that the Nikes I bought for my daughter had a hole after a month of wear. They refunded my entire purchase without me needing to return the shoes."

Why am I sharing all of these stories? To show that a number of companies—both B2C and B2B—are starting to figure this customer experience thing out. So if your company hasn't yet, you're behind the competition.

It's also to demonstrate that no matter what business you're in, you can create a remarkable and Extraordinary experience just by treating your customers the right way (like you'd want to be treated).

When you do the right thing for the customer, they often end up happier than if they hadn't had a problem in the first place.

What stood out to me about this Facebook exchange? The number of people who quickly recounted a great experience with a company and were more than willing to tell the story weeks, maybe months later.

☆ ☆ ☆ ☆ ☆

Sometimes the smallest changes in the customer experience have the biggest impact. It's the little things that often matter most to customers, and if they are consistent irritants, removing them can immediately improve the overall experience.

Many of these "little things" are there because they've always been there and no one has questioned them.

For example, who decided that ATMs could only dispense $20 bills?

PNC Bank changed its ATMs to allow customers to "Choose Your Bills." Now instead of being forced to accept the bills that the bank wants to give, customers can ask for—and receive—any combination of bills they choose.

It may sound like a small change, but it wasn't to customer Marianne Hynd, who told this story on the *Experience This!* podcast:

> *I'm a mom of three kids, and part of my weekly routine includes getting lunch money for school. As we know, ATMs typically like to distribute tens and twenties, which makes it difficult to divide out. So initially, I would take money from the ATM, but then I'd need to stop somewhere to make a small purchase so I could get some singles, which to be honest was kind of a pain and something I never look forward to.*
>
> *So a couple of years ago, PNC, which is who I bank with, did start allowing ATM withdrawals in multiples of a dollar, which was a really welcomed change, and while it did ease up the process a little bit, I still had to make three separate transactions. But I was OK with it at the time.*
>
> *However, I went to the ATM the other day, and started going through the process, and after choosing the amount for the withdrawal I saw three game-changing words: "Choose Your Bills."*
>
> *PNC now allows customers to choose which denominations they'd like for their withdrawals. Now this is such a small change, but I can't tell you how happy it made me. Probably happier than the folks at PNC intended! But really, what it did for me as a consumer is that it took one more step out of the process and it made my weekly trip a little bit quicker.*
>
> *I've been a customer of PNC for many years, and it's little changes like that that will keep me a customer for many years to come.*[81]

Chapter 9

RESPONSIVE

By now you have become WISE—Witty, Immersive, Shareable, Extraordinary—and know the ingredients needed to create remarkable customer experiences in your business.

But I would not be doing my job if you finished this book and were just WISE because, let's face it, your competition is probably somewhat wise too. I want you to be WISER than your competitors.

When you follow the WISE methodology, you'll find that more people are going to talk about your brand to their friends, their family, and on social media. So what's the final step? You must be Responsive to all of these newfound positive mentions.

It is truly a gift when people take time out of their day to compliment a company. As I noted previously, marketers call it "word of mouth," and it is the Holy Grail of marketing. But then when it happens, so many companies ignore it.

If I get offstage after a keynote and someone says, "Dan, that was an amazing presentation" and I just keep walking, that would be kind of rude, right? Yet companies ignore customers' compliments every single day. Being Responsive is the last part of the WISER methodology.

Chris Zane, founder and CEO of Zane's Cycles, said in 2011 that "customer service starts when the customer experience fails."[82] How right he is! If you want to stop people from calling customer service, make the customer experience perfect.

When customers do call, a critical moment presents itself—we can convert someone who is upset with us (because we delivered a *meh* experience or missed their expectations) into a happy customer for life.

The first rule of thumb? Serve the customer in the channel of *their* choice, not the channel of *your* choice.

If somebody called or emailed your company with a customer service question, would you tell them to tweet instead? Of course not.

So when people tweet at companies, why do so many of them tell the customer to call or email? That doesn't make any sense.

A customer tweets at your brand because that is their channel of choice. Chances are, they already know you have a toll-free phone number and an email address, but they chose not to use those channels (or maybe they did and didn't get a satisfactory answer). Don't tell them what channel you want them to use; it wouldn't happen in other channels, and it's not OK to do it in social media either.

Be aware that preferred channels have shifted over time, so companies must shift as well. According to Sitel Group, the telephone was the most popular channel for brand engagement as recently as 2018. But by 2020 it was in third place behind email and online chat, with social media not far behind.[83]

Secondly, set customer expectations about when you will be available to respond and how long a response usually takes. It's not necessary to offer 24/7 customer service if your customers aren't using your product or service at all hours, but it is definitely necessary to communicate your availability in order to manage expectations.

Brandwatch analyzed more than 200 million online conversations and surveyed thousands of people. They found that consumers who use social media (publicly or via private direct message) in a customer service scenario "were most likely to expect an answer within minutes," whereas most other customers said they "wanted a response within 24 hours" regardless of channel.[84]

Finally, don't be afraid of complaints. Customers who complain do so because they care; they genuinely want the company to know that it missed expectations, and importantly, they want to give it a chance to resolve the situation. If those customers didn't care, and most don't, they would simply leave for a competitor without saying a word.

Complaints are often more valuable than compliments because they tell a company how it is missing the mark in terms of customer experience. Often, complaints can identify hidden pain points or unintended barriers that once fixed can greatly improve customer satisfaction scores.

How a company responds to a complaint feeds right back into the overall perception of the brand experience:

"While customers know that mistakes can happen, they also expect companies to at least match their level of effort to resolve the problem," according to a study by Medallia and Ipsos. "Our research reveals that when consumers believe they have put in more effort than a company to resolve an issue, they are twice as likely to tell friends, family or colleagues about the bad experience, and four times more likely to stop purchasing from the company, switch brands, or use the company less."[85]

In other words, word-of-mouth marketing can go both ways—positively and negatively.

"Today's customers are quick both to penalize companies for negative experiences and to reward them for positive ones," the report continues. "They are also well aware that their influence in the marketplace is stronger than ever and are willing to use that influence to directly affect your brand's reputation, both for good and for ill."[86]

☆ ☆ ☆ ☆ ☆

The employees at Crock-Pot will likely never forget Sunday, February 4, 2018. It's not because it was Super Bowl Sunday, with the Eagles defeating the Patriots, 41-33. It's because of what happened afterward: perhaps the most memorable and emotional episode of the NBC show *This Is Us*.

I won't reveal any spoilers, but the episode contains one of the most critical scenes in the history of the series. The main character, Jack, is standing in the kitchen with the antagonist, which happens to be an old Crock-Pot on the counter. Now it's important to note that Crock-Pot, at the time this episode ran, did not have a Twitter presence at all.

The executives at Crock-Pot woke up Monday morning to thousands of tweets like this one:

Kayla N.
@kayNiedz

Follow ⌄

thanks to @NBCThisisUs for crushing my soul week after week. additionally, i'll no longer be making #crockpot chili after last night's episode.

10:03 AM - 24 Jan 2018

The Crock-Pot team jumped right on it; they created a Twitter handle, and they started answering as fast as they could:

The Crockpot® Brand ✓
@CrockPotCares

Replying to @kayNiedz and @NBCThisisUs

We're 💔 over last night's episode, too! Kayla, we're innocent until proven guilty. Since the '70s we've been providing families with quality & safe products, ask your parents if you don't believe us. DM us w/ any ?? & we'd be happy to tell you more about our safety standards!

12:58 PM · Jan 24, 2018 · Twitter Web Client

My favorite part is, "Ask your parents if you don't believe us" because it demonstrates that the company *knows* Kayla and which generation she represents.

Would you like to guess what Kayla does next? How about this?

Kayla N.
@kayNiedz

Follow ⌄

Replying to @CrockPotCares

I apologize for what I said when I was in an emotional state— I could never live without my beloved crockpot #crockpotisinnocent

8:40 PM - 24 Jan 2018

So Crock-Pot turned somebody who was angry at their brand into a brand lover *just by being Responsive.* I guarantee you Kayla didn't think Crock-Pot was going to respond to her. Now she loves the brand because it did.

☆ ☆ ☆ ☆ ☆

Duke Energy, a utility company mostly located in the southeastern United States, is essentially a monopoly. Yet the company often posts videos of their "Storm Director" on social media to tell people that storms are coming and to alert them that they may lose power.

How many companies do you know that are willing to advertise that their service is down, let alone *before* it is down?

By being proactively Responsive, Duke Energy's customers trust their utility company. They believe in the company and know that it is out there working for them in the midst of a power outage.

The best part is that when the storm does hit and the power does go out, the call center isn't overwhelmed because the company has prepared people. They've told them ahead of time, and people believe that they're on the case.

"People in those situations feel like we're there for them, we're prepared," said Duke Energy's Madeleine Piercy. "I think it helps build confidence in our brand, that we are giving them the tools they need to stay safe and be prepared."[87]

One company I worked for often learned from Twitter that its website was down. In other words, customers on Twitter noticed it before the IT department.

Even then, the company's public relations team was hesitant to get out in front of the problem for fear of bad press. But you know what? A social media post that says, "We know our website is down, we're working on it, and we'll get it back up just as soon as we can" will stop the influx of complaints and customer service phone calls. It will also gain trust.

☆ ☆ ☆ ☆ ☆

The social media team at Puffs Tissues saw this tweet from Leandra one evening in November 2019:

Leandra
@Lomarie07   ⌄

How did I manage to celebrate my 30th birthday? With @Mucinex and @Puffs 😄 Thanks for all the happy birthday wishes, I'll be sleeping for the next day now. #thisis30

9:42 PM · Nov 2, 2019 · Twitter for iPhone

The company responded with this great tweet:

Puffs ✔
@Puffs   ⌄

Replying to @Lomarie07

Looks like you didn't plan on inviting us to your birthday "party" but we're happy we could help out in some way, Leandra! 🎂 Happy belated, and we hope you're feeling better. Could you send us a quick DM after your slumber? 😉

10:10 AM · Nov 4, 2019 · Sprinklr

Leandra responded with "You guys are too sweet" and of course sent the company a direct message.

A couple of weeks later, she received a package in the mail along with a handwritten note. Leandra immediately went back to Twitter with a photo of the package's gift-wrapped contents (Puffs tissues, natch) and the note. Her tweet read:

Leandra
@Lomarie07

Let's talk about brands showing up for their customers. After @Puffs found out I was sick on my birthday, they sent a HANDWRITTEN personalized card and a bunch of tissues to get me through the rest of cold season. @dgingiss, @Hyken check this out! 💕

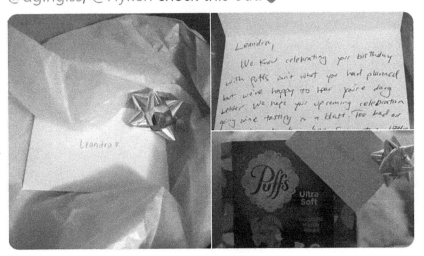

8:15 AM · Nov 21, 2019 · Twitter for iPhone

A happy customer shares kudos to the brand to all of her friends and followers. Isn't this the kind of word-of-mouth marketing that marketers stay up nights dreaming about? All it took was some social listening and being Responsive.

By the way, did you notice that Leandra tagged me and my friend Shep Hyken in the tweet? She knows we are both customer experience speakers, and I'm guessing she hoped we'd get the word out a little bit more about her experience. Well, her story appeared on my podcast and now here she is in my book. Great job, Puffs!

When Taylor Sipes reached out to Southwest Airlines with this tweet, she probably wasn't expecting much:

Taylor Sipes
@taylorsipes7

@SouthwestAir help!! My friend is in a wedding on Saturday in Costa Rica but she left her bridesmaid dress here in Houston! Can we get her dress on flight #1734 tomorrow??? #WorthATry #BestCustomerService

6:57 PM · Feb 28, 2019 · Twitter for iPhone

Taylor isn't anyone famous; in fact, she only has 299 followers on Twitter as of this writing. There is no evidence she was even a Southwest customer when she wrote the tweet, although I'm betting she is now. She had chosen the airline because she knew they had a flight the next day to the wedding destination.

Less than two hours later, Southwest responded to her, asking for her friend's contact information. Another two hours later, and the plan was set in motion. Southwest retweeted Taylor's tweet with the comment, "Alright, let's do it!"

Southwest Airlines ✔
@SouthwestAir

Alright, let's do it!

🔘 **Taylor Sipes** @taylorsipes7 · Feb 28, 2019
@SouthwestAir help!! My friend is in a wedding on Saturday in Costa Rica but she left her bridesmaid dress here in Houston! Can we get her dress on flight #1734 tomorrow??? #WorthATry #BestCustomerService
Show this thread

9:37 PM · Feb 28, 2019 · Twitter for iPhone

744 Retweets   **427** Quote Tweets   **8.1K** Likes

Thus began a series of movements (and tweets) from Southwest that allowed the entire world to follow the flight's route using the hashtag #RescueTheDress.

Online, pictures appeared of the dress's arrival at the originating airport, being checked as baggage, and arriving at its destination, along with a flight tracker to view its progress in real time. Several Southwest employees appeared in the photos along with the dress protagonists.

The Twitterverse ate it up; Southwest's tweets each received thousands of likes, and the airline received hundreds of positive comments from onlookers.

Did being Responsive cost Southwest any money? Not really; they were flying the plane anyway, and they just had to add a dress to the cargo. They turned a social listening opportunity into a huge public relations win leveraging their existing systems, with national coverage in *USA Today*, Fox News, and the *Today* show. You can't buy that kind of marketing.

☆ ☆ ☆ ☆ ☆

My friend Stephanie Baiocchi experienced a pizza crisis on New Year's Eve. She wanted to have pizza delivered so she took to social media to ask her favorite brand whether they were going to be open on New Year's Eve.

Now as a former pizza delivery driver, I know that New Year's Eve is a high-volume pizza night; I'll never forget the time I delivered to a big party and the host literally handed a hat around the room for my tip!

Needless to say, the company confirmed that it would be open after checking Stephanie's zip code.

It turns out her question wasn't crazy, though. New Year's Eve arrived, and Stephanie tried to order her pizza via the mobile app, which was not working.

Stephanie tweeted a screenshot of the malfunctioning app (remember when I said there is no such thing as an offline experience anymore?) to the pizza brand:

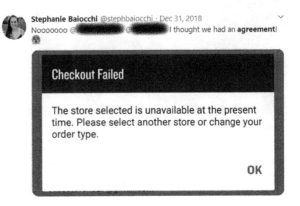

She didn't receive a response, so she did what so many customers do—she went to the competition. Unbelievably, that company's app wasn't working either.

Stephanie then did the only other thing she could think of—she walked into her kitchen, opened up the freezer, and pulled out a frozen DiGiorno pizza.

Naturally, she then tweeted a photo of herself and her husband eating the DiGiorno pizza (another offline experience coming online), and she even managed to throw in a reference to DiGiorno's tagline:

Stephanie Baiocchi
@stephbaiocchi

Welp. @DiGiorno ftw. It's not delivery (cause nothing was open) but Digiorno to the rescue.

For those not in the know, "ftw" stands for "for the win," and DiGiorno's popular tagline is: "It's not delivery. It's DiGiorno."

Stephanie's tweet was posted at one minute before midnight Eastern Standard Time in the US. A little more than an hour later, a frozen pizza company did what two national pizza delivery companies couldn't do: It responded.

All DiGiorno did was be Responsive, and the company made a fan for life.

Even billionaire Elon Musk has been known to personally respond to customers' Tesla questions on Twitter just as Amazon founder Jeff Bezos shares his email address for customers to use.

If they can do it, so can you.

Being Responsive in the channel of the customer's choice means being available in multiple places, sometimes even in evolving service channels.

When I arrived at The Hyatt Confidante in Miami, the receptionist recommended that I text them with any needs during my stay. He said that you couldn't always automatically reach someone on the guest services phone number, and, of course, the front desk was often helping other guests. But the text line, he said, was open twenty-four hours a day, seven days a week, and usually had a response time of just a couple of minutes because every hotel employee could access it.

I hadn't thought of texting a hotel, but I was willing to try it. During the stay, though, I forgot all about the text line. So at one point, I stood in line at the front desk to ask about getting additional bottles of water for my room. I waited patiently while the receptionist checked in a new guest, and when the receptionist finally helped me, he said, "You didn't have to wait in line! You could have just texted."

I thought that was so interesting, so I investigated a little more.

According to Slalom Build, which led the design and user experience for Hyatt's mobile app:

"Hyatt recognized that travelers don't like to ask for things and will often go without if it's not easy to do. With the World of Hyatt app, you can check in, check out, text the concierge, order in-room dining and other services, and even request hospitality items to be delivered to your room. Need some coffee, another pillow, or some extra towels? Forget your toothbrush or razor? Not only can you request these items (and more), the app lets you check delivery status and timing."[88]

Slalom and Hyatt collaborated on what was referred to as "digital hospitality" to achieve three goals:

1. Increase engagement and improve guest experience from booking through post-departure.
2. Gain better insight into guest needs and preferences, and use this to continue to enhance their future experiences with Hyatt.
3. Build a flexible, scalable, digital platform that enables industry-leading features.[89]

The key takeaway is that if you can remove a customer pain point (having to ask for things) and make it incredibly easy (just send a text) you can avoid negative experiences and show your customers that you are Responsive to their needs.

☆ ☆ ☆ ☆ ☆

A nine-year-old girl named Riley Morrison sent a handwritten letter to NBA All-Star and league MVP Stephen "Steph" Curry. It read:

> Dear Stephen Curry,
> My name is Riley (Just like your daughter). I'm 9 years old from Napa, California. I am a big fan of yours. I enjoy going to Warriors games with my dad. I asked my dad to buy me the new Curry 5's, because I'm starting a new basketball season. My dad and I visited the Under Armour website and were disappointed to see that there were no Curry 5's for sale under the girls [sic] section. However, they did have them for sale under the boy's [sic] section, even to customize. I know you support girl athletes because you have two daughters and you host an all girls basketball camp. I hope you can work with Under Armour to change this because girls want to rock the Curry 5's too.
> Sincerely,
> Riley Morrison

I don't know about you, but I got the chills when I read this letter. Any athlete or celebrity or company in the world would pay to get a letter like this from a true fan.

The best part, though, is that Steph Curry didn't disappoint in his response, which was also a handwritten letter:

> Hey Riley,
> I appreciate your concern and have spent the last 2 days talking to Under Armour about how we can fix the issue. Unfortunately, we

have labeled smaller sizes as "Boys" on the website. We are correcting this <u>now!</u> I want to make sure you can wear my kicks proudly—so I'm going to send you a pair of Curry 5's now and you'll be one of the first kids to get the Curry 6. Lastly, we have something special in the works for International Women's Day on March 8th, and I want you to celebrate with me! More to come on that, but plan on being in Oakland that night! All the best! #RuinTheGame

— Stephen

Darren Rovell ✔
@darrenrovell

Girl named Riley Morrison asks @StephenCurry30 why his sneakers don't come in girls sizes. Steph responds.

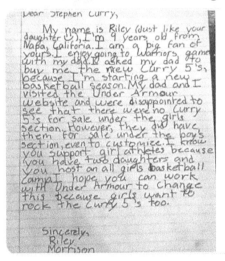

Dear Stephen Curry,

My name is Riley (just like your daughter ☺), I'm 9 years old from Napa, California. I am a big fan of yours. I enjoy going to Warriors games with my dad. I asked my dad to buy me the new Curry 5's, because I'm starting a new basketball season. My dad and I visited the Under Armour website and were disappointed to see that there were no Curry 5's for sale under the girls section, however, they did have them for sale under the boys section, even to customize. I know you support girl athletes because you have two daughters and you host an all girls basketball camp. I hope you can work with Under Armour to change this because girls want to rock the Curry 5's too.

Sincerely,
Riley Morrison

Hey Riley,

I appreciate your concern and have spent the last 2 days talking to Under Armour about how we can fix the issue. Unfortunately, we have labeled smaller sizes as "boys" on the website. We are correcting this now! I want to make sure you can wear my kicks proudly - so I am going to send you a pair of Curry 5's now and you'll be one of the first kids to get the Curry 6. Lastly, we have something special in the works for International Women's Day on March 8th, and I want you to celebrate with me! More to come on that, but plan to be in Oakland that night! All the best!
#RuinTheGame

- Stephen

10:08 AM · Nov 29, 2018 · Twitter for iPhone

43.4K Retweets **10.7K** Quote Tweets **210.7K** Likes

Wow! Could you get any more Responsive than that? It turns out that the Curry 6's were sold in a "United We Win" design in girls' sizes, with a sockliner designed by Morrison herself.

Darren Rovell ✔
@darrenrovell

4 months ago, Riley Morrison, 9, wrote a letter to Steph Curry asking why the Currys weren't in girl sizes. He said he'd change it. Tomorrow, on International Women's Day, Under Armour is selling the Curry 6 "United We Win, in girl's sizes, with a sockliner designed by Morrison!

6:39 PM · Mar 7, 2019 · Twitter for iPhone

Incidentally, the first tweet about this story, shared by former ESPN contributor Darren Rovell, garnered more than 210,000 likes and more than 54,000 retweets—pretty good branding for Mr. Curry and Under Armour.

Now if Stephen Curry, multimillionaire NBA All-Star, can respond to a customer's handwritten letter, can't we all do the same?

Being Responsive to customers shows them—and others—that you care. Responding to everyone, whether they are complaining, complimenting, or simply inquiring, should be a consistent business practice because that is what today's customers expect.

"Consumers' relationships with brands are not all that different from relationships with people. Some you genuinely care about, while others are in your life simply because you depend on them," according to *Business News Daily*. "Marketers who realize this will be in a better position to retain customers and improve the perceptions of consumers who are unhappy with a brand's service or product."[90]

Remembering the Sitel Group's research regarding customers' willingness to share positive experiences more than negatives ones, it becomes clear that simply responding to a customer can *become* that positive experience.

There are countless examples of customers who start off as brand detractors because of a disappointing experience and end up as brand advocates because of a great response.

Brandwatch looked at the best brands for customer experience and noted that "those that get the most positivity tend to have built out a large community with deep ties to the brands."[91]

The top-ranked brands in the study were Etsy, MTV, Sephora, Four Seasons Hotels, Dior, GameStop, Kia, Wendy's, Chanel, and Dove.

Etsy, the e-commerce site focused on handmade gifts, "has created a fantastic community of passionate creators and fans of custom, handmade items," says Brandwatch. "Meanwhile, MTV's fans have remained loyal for a long time and speak of the brand like an old friend."

"These long-standing (sometimes emotional) ties can be good for building a strong network of brand advocates," the report concludes.[92]

To become better at being Responsive, make sure your company is:

- Listening to your customers in all channels
- Viewing complaints as opportunities to improve
- Identifying common questions or web searches that may be barriers
- Fixing what's wrong with the experience to avoid future complaints

Chapter 10

IMPLEMENTING WISER AT YOUR COMPANY

Hopefully, the examples and case studies in this book have inspired you to create remarkable experiences at your company that your customers will want to share. The challenge, then, is how to get started.

Having worked in Corporate America for twenty years, I know it can be difficult if not impossible to get everyone aligned on an idea, let alone agreeing on requirements, getting the project prioritized, gaining legal approval, and executing it in the marketplace.

According to eMarketer, "While each supporting actor in an organization may have a slightly different view on customer experience, to 'get it right,' everyone must align on the overarching goals and visions of delivering that experience."[93]

Complicating matters is the fact that senior executives are often unaware of the challenges that the "worker bees" face every day.

At one of my former employers, a bunch of us were tasked with creating a humorous video to open up an employee awards ceremony. The video followed a fictional young, overly ambitious intern and his hopelessly optimistic manager. It showed them as they weaved their way through all of the meetings and checkpoints throughout the organization in an attempt to launch a new product.

Every meeting was intentionally a caricature but adhered to that infamous quote of Homer Simpson: "It's funny 'cuz it's true."

Sure enough, the audience roared with laughter as the intern had to write pages and pages of documentation for the technology team and convince the brand team that the new product was "on brand." They kept laughing as he rolled his eyes at the legal team's insistence that he add 500 words of disclosures to a 100-word marketing flyer.

One person, however, wasn't laughing. After the video ended, the CEO turned to one of his VPs and asked, "Is it really like that?"

"No marketing department or CMO will be successful in pursuing and executing customer experience efforts unless the CEO and executive teams are completely on board," according to eMarketer.[94]

That's why the examples in this book are simple, practical, and inexpensive. While this won't eliminate all of the barriers you're bound to face in executing your ideas, it should make the process faster and easier.

Remember that customer experience isn't a "project"; it's a way of thinking that needs to be ingrained in the culture of the company. In other words, it's a marathon, not a sprint, so don't try to solve everything at once.

"Achieving customer experience 'perfection' is not an attainable goal—at least not in today's environment," states eMarketer. "While total perfection isn't possible, mastering select aspects of the customer experience is."[95]

It is also not necessary to incorporate all of the letters of WISER into every experience; often just one or two of them will suffice in creating a differentiated experience. But the more letters you incorporate, the better your customers will perceive the experience and the harder time your competitors will have copying it.

Always start with what the customer wants. Customer data can help you determine that. Be sure to differentiate between VOC ("voice of the customer") and what I call AOC ("actions of the customer"). This is critical because what customers *say* (VOC) and what customers *do* (AOC) are not always the same.

VOC and AOC data can help determine which WISER letters are most important to your customers.

The following chapters outline four steps to implementing WISER in your organization: Eliminating pain points/friction, designing the right digital experience, adapting to changing trends in the contact center, and solidifying executive leadership with a CXO (chief experience officer).

Chapter 11

ELIMINATING PAIN POINTS/FRICTION

According to *Harvard Business Review*, the number-one most important factor in a customer's loyalty is reducing customer effort.[96] Think about that every day. Think about how you can make your customers' lives easier. Do that, and you will create loyalty.

You can't expect your customers to know everything. Yes, today's customers are more connected and have access to more information than any other generation of customers in history, but they still can't read minds (at least not yet). So why do many companies create situations where customers need to figure things out for themselves?

The following stories actually happened to me and illustrate how to reduce customer effort.

When I upgraded my phone, I had to re-login to most of the phone's applications. Some apps are linked to the physical device, so I also had to update that indicator in several cases.

This was mostly an easy process, except for one app: the commuter train line that I used to take to work. I had previously purchased some ten-ride ticket packages, and when I logged into the app with my new phone, they were gone.

After trying and failing several times to fix the problem on my own, I contacted the company through the app. About twenty-four hours later, I received a phone call from a lovely "Miss Jackson," who proceeded to reinstate my tickets with no questions asked.

"This happens when people switch phones," she said matter-of-factly, which surprised me a bit. The company knew this was an issue but hadn't bothered to fix it. Instead, it relied on customers contacting customer service to ultimately have the tickets manually reinstated.

This is what's called a "known error," which *Wikipedia* defines as "software bugs which have yet to be fixed but have a known root cause and either have little disruptive impact on the end user or a known work around."[97]

Let's dissect this definition as it pertains to my experience:

- This is indeed a "software bug" that has "yet to be fixed," and logging in to see nearly $100 in tickets gone was not a good customer experience.
- The bug has a "known root cause": customers switching devices. Unfortunately, this is not a rare occurrence, as millions of customers do that every year.
- The bug did not have "little disruptive impact on the end user." I had to wait some twenty-four hours (and purchase additional tickets in the meantime for my daily commute) and move to a different channel than what I preferred.
- There was a "known work around": me having to talk with Miss Jackson on the phone to get the problem resolved.

As nice and helpful as Miss Jackson was, this is not an acceptable work-around, especially for an issue that is likely to surface on an annual basis with people upgrading their phones so often. By fixing the root cause of the problem, the company can vastly improve the customer experience and free up Miss Jackson to handle other customer service issues.

I experienced another, similar issue with the same phone upgrade but with a different company.

I purchased the new phone at a major wireless company's retail store, and at the same time I purchased an OtterBox case (OtterBox, incidentally, gets customer experience right, as I highlighted in *Winning at Social Customer Care*).

When I got home, excited to try out the new phone and protect it with the new case, I realized that I had purchased the wrong-sized case. I blamed myself for not checking the package carefully, but in the next breath, I wondered why the salesperson let me leave the store without confirming that I'd bought the right-sized case.

This should have been an easy catch for someone who spends all day working with phones and cases.

Proactive customer service can be a game-changer for customers and the companies with which they do business. Anticipating customers' needs makes them feel like you're looking out for them, that they are safe and secure in your hands. Forcing them to figure out their own mistakes creates the opposite effect.

Incidentally, the commuter train line that flubbed the phone upgrade does have a genius method for anticipating customers' needs: When trains arrive late into the downtown train station, representatives on hand pass out "late slips" to passengers who may be concerned about not arriving to work on time. The "Train Delay Notice" says simply:

> *To Whom It May Concern:*
> *This is to advise that trains were unavoidably delayed due to difficulties encountered in Suburban Service today.*
> *If you require additional information, or to verify this notice, please contact Passenger Services at [phone number].*
> *We apologize for any inconvenience this may have caused.*
> *Thank you.*

Back to the phone case. After walking a mile from my downtown office to another retail location of the same wireless provider (I had made the original purchase in the suburbs), a representative told me I had to return the item at the same store where I purchased it—a completely unnecessary and customer-unfriendly inconvenience.

By the time I got around to returning the case, I had already purchased the correct size on (you guessed it) Amazon with same-day delivery. That was a lost sale to the wireless provider. It could have been avoided had the salesperson been proactively looking out for the customer.

Whenever possible, don't make customers do extra work. If there is a "known error" in your process, either fix it immediately or communicate to customers proactively. If you see a customer about to make a mistake, do whatever you can to help them prevent it.

Imagine how my experience would have been different if the commuter rail app had popped up a message that said, "We see you have a new device. Let's help you find your tickets." Or if the wireless provider salesperson had simply asked, "Are you sure you want to buy this case? It doesn't fit your new phone."

These are simple fixes, but they go a long way toward reducing customer effort and creating a more positive customer experience.

Case Study: Discover Card

Discover Card is a leading credit card issuer in the United States and also my employer from 2006 to 2015. My last role there, from April 2013 to November 2015, was head of digital customer experience and social media. During my tenure in that role, we launched many new digital initiatives and features, but we also used VOC and AOC data to identify and eliminate customer pain points.

From cardmember behavioral data (AOC), Discover learned that the desire to check on recent transactions was a top reason people logged in to the website. Qualitative research (VOC) confirmed this trend, with customers saying they just wanted to ensure they were getting charged what they thought they were getting charged (i.e., the waiter at the restaurant didn't add on an extra tip).

The problem? It was too difficult to access recent transactions on the website. It wasn't immediately clear where to go, and the user had to click two or three times to get there.

Discover's answer? Create a Facebook-like feed on the homepage which contained the latest ten card transactions. So as soon as customers logged in, they saw their balance due, their rewards balance, and the last ten transactions they had made on the card.

Almost immediately, an amazing thing happened: Hundreds of thousands of customers logged in, didn't click anything, and logged off.

An e-commerce retailer would call that phenomenon a "bounce," which Google Analytics defines as "a single-page session on your site . . . calculated specifically as a session that triggers only a single request to the Analytics server, such as when a user opens a single page on your site and then exits without triggering any other requests to the Analytics server during that session."[98]

Generally, "bounce rate" is considered a negative score as it is a measure of site relevancy. But since this was a private page (one behind the login page), the change did not affect search engine results.

At Discover, we celebrated the high "bounce rate" because we knew the change had delivered exactly what customers wanted. They were immediately logging out because *they had found what they were looking for* almost immediately.

Customer satisfaction scores for the website skyrocketed, and not coincidentally, that was the year Discover won the coveted J.D. Power Award for Customer Satisfaction—the results of which depend heavily on website interactions—for the first time in the survey's existence.[99]

One thing that Discover understood: People don't want to visit their credit card website. So when they have to, they want the experience to be over as fast as possible. Unless you are Starbucks or Disney or Netflix, chances are that is true about your website too.

Discover also used a survey widget on every page of its website. It allowed users to click on a feedback icon, score their interaction, and leave comments. We received dozens and sometimes hundreds of comments every day, with tens of millions of customers logging in monthly or more often.

This "voice of the customer" (VOC) feedback was compiled into a report that was distributed every day to the digital team and various other executives.

The report made it easy to identify urgent issues that needed addressing immediately because many similar comments would appear on the same day. But it was harder to see more infrequent trends that maybe only showed up every few days with one or two customers complaining.

To address this, we added a single question to each survey: "How easy was it to use the Discover Card website today?" The quantitative question, answered on a scale of one to seven, was based on the Forrester Customer Experience Index. Forrester previously asked a similar question on the brand level in its surveys as one of three key components of an annual ranking (Forrester has since changed its methodology).

After about six weeks of collecting the data, I asked for a report listing every page of the website (there were thousands) in order of the average ease-of-use score. Immediately, I turned to the back page and looked at the pages with the worst scores—in other words, the ones that customers said made it most difficult to use the Discover site.

The absolute bottom-ranking page turned out to be a very important one—the "Refer a Friend" page where cardmembers could enter the names and email addresses of their friends and earn $50 each for them and their friend if the friend signed up for a Discover Card.

I then dug into the recent customer comments from just that page, and a previously unidentified trend surfaced immediately: On one particular browser, the "Submit" button was not displaying.

Imagine asking customers to recommend their friends, having them enter names and email addresses, and then not being able to submit them!

As the head of digital customer experience, I was mortified. The fix was quick and easy from a technology perspective, and immediately thereafter, the Refer a Friend page's ease-of-use scores returned to normal.

What I did next took some people by surprise: I ran through the same exercise for the bottom 100 pages.

We found so many little pain points that were easy to fix but had enormous impact on customer satisfaction scores—and the J.D. Power survey.

One trick that worked well with the technology team: asking to "borrow" a programmer for two weeks to focus on all of these small changes, which together added up to a decent-sized project with significant impact. Otherwise, we would have never gotten a bunch of small fixes prioritized against larger projects.

☆ ☆ ☆ ☆ ☆

Indeed, this method can work across channels.

"Collecting customer feedback makes a difference," says GetFeedback. "For the best results, businesses should collect feedback from key touch points across the journey map through all feasible communication channels."[100]

GetFeedback also notes: "The most common use of customer feedback is simply to resolve CX issues (87%). This 'find-and-fix' paradigm is a common and often necessary place to start with CX programs but there are many more strategic ways to use customer feedback. For instance, improving the product and identifying trends were popular uses for a majority of respondents. Feedback can also be used to find ways to identify customers at risk for defection (47%)."[101]

The "find-and-fix" method is not universally applauded. Chip and Dan Heath, authors of *The Power of Moments*, a best-selling and seminal book on customer experience, said in an interview with Heart of the Customer's Jim Tincher:

> *The payoff for building peaks is much larger than the payoff for fixing potholes. We did a study with Forrester Research, using the data from their massive annual CX Index survey. And part of that survey is to ask consumers how they felt about their last experience with a certain brand (Dell, Southwest Airlines, Progressive Insurance, and so on). The consumers provide a score from 1 (very bad) to 7 (very good).*
>
> *So imagine that you were the CCO of one of those brands, and you get this data. Some customers are happy with you and some aren't. In response, we give you the option to choose one of two plans. Plan A would be to eliminate the negatives: You could move all your 1s, 2s, and 3s up to a 4. Plan B would be to elevate the positives: You could move all your 4s, 5s, and 6s up to a 7. Which would you choose?*
>
> *Here's the surprise: Plan B is 8.8 times more valuable in dollar terms than Plan A! Why is that true? Two reasons: There are way more mildly positive customers (4s, 5s, and 6s) than dissatisfied customers, and also, the more a customer likes you, the most he/she spends.*
>
> *The further surprise is that, when we asked executives at well-respected service companies how they spend their time, they estimated that they spent 80 percent on eliminating the negatives. We're spending the great majority of our time on the less valuable path!*
>
> *That's a huge opportunity. Just by reallocating some time from potholes to peaks, we can achieve big gains.*[102]

The Heath brothers are certainly not wrong. In fact, their strategy has also been validated in the Human Resources realm with the skills of individual employees. The well-known StrengthsFinder test, now known as CliftonStrengths, rates individuals across thirty-four themes based on the answers to 177 questions. The recommendation is then for the individual to focus on building up their strengths rather than improving their weaknesses.

Indeed, focusing on improving one's strengths—or going from *Good to Great,* as best-selling author Jim Collins calls it, is far more effective than trying to improve one's weaknesses. After all, *Horrible to Fair* wouldn't have been nearly as memorable a book title!

My perspective is that both "building peaks" and "fixing potholes" are important, and the potholes part can usually be done more quickly and with less expense.

Eliminating pain points can move some 1s to 6s or 7s, and even though there are fewer of them, this is what plugs the "leaky bucket" and prevents people from leaving your business just because of a single bad experience. Recall the statistics at the beginning of this book that demonstrated how quickly customers do this.

It also helps convince management, with data, that improving customer experience works *vis-à-vis* the metrics they care about.

In the case of Discover, the company would not have won the J.D. Power Award without having eliminated so many customer pain points.

Tom Karinshak, EVP and chief customer experience officer of Comcast, agrees. I asked him how much of his job is innovating new experiences versus trying to fix existing pain points that are known problems.

"It's a balance," he said. "You want to be able to take care of the immediate needs right now, as well as being focused on the future."[103]

In the customer journey, pain points are likely to occur whenever there is a transition or handoff from one department to another. This doesn't just mean when a customer service call is transferred to another department; it can occur whenever a customer is passed from one part of the organization to a different part of the organization.

The most common yet preventable example? When a customer is passed from a salesperson to an "account manager" or "customer success" associate. Think about it: As consumers, we buy from people we like. How, then, are we supposed to feel when that person we like immediately ditches us after the sale?

Imagine if you met the partner of your dreams, dated for a long time, and decided to get married. Then right at the part of the wedding where you exchange the rings, your partner thanks you for dating him/her and passes you on to his "associate" who will take the relationship from there?

This hypothetical story may sound outlandish, yet it happens every single day to consumers and businesses that buy from someone they like, only to be serviced by someone else.

According to eMarketer, "72% of internet users worldwide say a disconnected experience would make them change service providers/brands," where a disconnected experience was defined as "failing to know my preferences across all the touchpoints I engage with and are unable to provide access to information I need within a timely manner."[104]

The ill-conceived handoff between a salesperson and another employee often creates that feeling of being "disconnected." Does the new account manager know the terms of the deal and details that were discussed with the salesperson? Are they going to deliver on all of the salesperson's promises?

Salespeople continue to be incentivized on one key metric: new customers in the system. Marketing often operates separately, focusing on upper-funnel activities like brand awareness or acting just as a support staff for sales. And customer service? They're not even involved in the sales process.

The problem with this setup? While it might make sense for the company, it doesn't make sense for the customer. The customer wants a consistent experience and one that persists beyond the sale. He or she doesn't care how your company is organized.

So let's back up for a moment and look at the sales process as an integral part of the customer/client experience—and one that is often the source of pain points.

The average manager or director at a Fortune 500 company receives seventy to 100-plus emails every day. I should know as I spent nearly twenty years in Corporate America. I would estimate that 20 to 40 percent of the entire job of a manager or director is answering emails.

So how do salespeople effectively use this marketing channel to break through and get a budget owner's attention? The most important thing is to avoid the two pitfalls of every other sales email: Sales emails all sound the same, and follow-up emails are incredibly annoying.

Sales Emails All Sound the Same

As a client, it sometimes feels like all salespeople attend the same salesperson training session, something like "How to Write the Perfect Email That Will Generate More Sales." But when your email sounds just like everyone else's, it is actually far from perfect.

Try to avoid these five overused phrases:

- 💡 "In your role as [insert title here] at [insert company name here], you must . . .": This introduction is terrific if the goal is to communicate that you know how to perform a mail merge and are blasting the same email to as many people as possible.

- 💡 "Just 15 minutes of your time": No sales meeting ever has taken only fifteen minutes, and your email recipient knows that all too well. Set reasonable expectations.

- 💡 "My VP/CFO/CEO will be in town . . .": This line is supposed to make the recipient think they are so important that only a top executive should be meeting with them. But it's putting the cart before the horse; if the target doesn't know you or your company, he or she isn't yet ready to talk with your executives.

- 💡 "We will help you grow your business": If your product or service isn't going to grow someone's business (either by producing more revenue or garnering cost savings), then you have no reason to be soliciting in the first place.

- 💡 "We work with all these great brands [insert logos here]": Multiple times I called friends at the brands listed and almost every time they had no idea who the vendor was. It gets to the point where every logo page looks the same, so it loses the impact. Instead, share actual customer reviews of your product or service.

Follow-up Emails Are Incredibly Annoying

The same salesperson training manual teaches that you must contact a prospect "X" many times before you can expect a response. That may be true, but it surely doesn't mean you need to use the same channel and repeat the same message multiple times.

In fact, that is the fastest way to get someone to hit the "spam" or "block" button in their email program.

Here are some "friendly reminder" email phrases that will cause immediate eye rolls:

- 💡 "Just checking to see if you got my email below?": There are only two possible answers to this question: Yes, in which case the person chose to not read it or to ignore it; or no, in which case this second email isn't going to be received either.

- 💡 "Bringing this to the top of your inbox": Not only does your target not want you messing with his or her inbox, but the mere idea that your email is so important it should be on "the top" is laughable considering that this entire communication is much more important to the salesperson than it is to the recipient.

- 💡 "You must not have responded because you were getting chased by a [insert wild animal here].": The first time I saw this as part of a multiple-choice follow-up email guessing at why I hadn't responded, I thought it was clever. By the twentieth time, I just sighed and hit delete.

One other annoying habit that must be avoided: Sending the same email to dozens of colleagues at the same company. Invariably what happens is that anyone who opens the email forwards it to the correct person, who has already received it once and now gets to receive it dozens more times.

The best way to stand out from the countless other vendors approaching the same target is not to follow the old salesperson playbook but to be intentionally different. Do that, and prospects will think twice before hitting delete.

Consider these three methods:

Personalize the Pitch

It doesn't take much effort to learn something about your prospect before sending a sales email.

Just like a warm introduction from a trusted colleague is more effective than a cold call, an introductory email that demonstrates you took the time to learn something about the prospect can be highly effective.

Perform a simple Google search and take a few minutes to read what you find. Then use that information in your email:

- 💡 "I read your recent post . . .": Whenever someone has read my book or *Forbes* articles, listened to my podcast, or seen one of my tweets, they immediately have my attention. I'm thankful for their engagement and interested in their feedback. The interaction feels genuine and not just like a cold sales pitch.
- 💡 "I noticed you're a huge baseball fan . . .": I could talk about baseball all day, so it's a good way to get my attention. It's also not a business-oriented topic, which is often a relief after sifting through dozens of other more "we will help you grow your business" emails.
- 💡 "I see you went to [insert university name here]. I have a funny story about that school . . .": People are usually very loyal to their *alma mater(s)*, so if you can base a conversation around their school, you'll often get their attention.

Provide Immediate Value

The best way to demonstrate the value of a product or service? Show instead of tell. This is especially true of digital-only services like SaaS platforms. If you can demonstrate that you understand the problems and challenges your prospect is trying to solve, you are much more likely to pique their interest. Then take it a step further and show the person what to expect.

When I led global social media at McDonald's, a social media analytics vendor emailed me a sample report with real data comparing the recent social media engagement levels of McDonald's, Burger King, and Wendy's. It was just a snapshot, but it communicated exactly what the service would provide. This was more effective than any email description could have been, and in fact I responded to the email because the report interested me.

Use Snail Mail

Email is fast, easy, and inexpensive. Snail mail is none of those things. But it stands out in a big way because most people receive little or no snail mail at work. When they do, the open rate is almost 100 percent, especially if it's thicker than a letter.

Consider these simple ideas that don't have to cost a lot of money:

- 💡 A book on a relevant topic
- 💡 A small, personalized item (not just a promotional item with your company logo)
- 💡 A handwritten note or card (see the Punkpost example)

Often, a personal item sent via snail mail will motivate a prospect to respond if for no reason other than guilt. It can be a genuine conversation starter compared to email, which almost always feels cold.

One vendor sent me a hardcover book written by his company's CEO. I had previously used this company at a different job. The experience was horrendous, so no way was I going to consider working with the company again. Had the salesperson merely emailed me, I would have ignored him. But since he sent me a book, I felt obliged to respond. He took the rejection well and even thanked me for saving him the time to follow up with me!

Another vendor got creative and sent me a bottle of wine that was locked with a device requiring a four-digit passcode. "Call me for the code so you can enjoy the wine," a note said. Clever! But alas, after leaving the bottle on my desk for a while, so many passersby tried the lock that eventually someone cracked the code and we all enjoyed the wine anyway!

Case Study: Windows versus Cars

This is a tale of two sales. Both are for big-ticket items, and both occurred after much research and comparison shopping. In one, the buyer has become a lifelong brand advocate; in the other, he has buyer's remorse. What happened?

One customer finally acknowledged the inevitable: His house needed new windows. Salesperson after salesperson came to the house, and he sat through what seemed like the exact same sales pitch for everyone. His favorite line: "Your cats will be so confused! They'll go sit in the sunlight and not feel any warmth!" (That turned out to be a false claim.)

He decided on a major national window retailer—all wood windows to maintain or increase the value of the house—mostly because he liked the salesperson. And for thirty-one windows, he thought, the salesperson had better have liked him too!

The installers arrived, and they were great—friendly, considerate, and efficient, and they cleaned up after themselves. He tipped them generously. The only problem? Four of the ground-floor windows that were supposed to be tempered by code (safer because they can better withstand that wayward baseball) arrived nontempered. So, the installation failed the requisite town inspection.

The installers apologized and promised to return with the right windows once they were ordered and produced.

A week or so later, the customer opened his door to find a different set of installers; as he found out later, they were the repair team, not the installation team. (As the customer, he didn't feel like his windows were completely "installed" yet because he hadn't received the right windows.) This team also showed up with nontempered windows, so he had to send them away.

Two weeks after that, a third crew arrived. It's important to note here that the customer had now stayed home from work three times to open his home to work crews. The moment he opened the door this time, he looked at the foreman's face and knew something was wrong.

"Let me guess," he said, "you have nontempered windows in your truck."

"Yes," the foreman replied sheepishly. The customer sent him away as well.

At this point, the customer tried calling the salesperson because the installation experience had left him more than a little bit frustrated. The salesperson promised to look into it, but he never called back. The customer then called the customer service line and demanded a refund for the four tempered windows that he never received, but they denied the request.

Finally, after another three weeks of waiting, a fourth crew arrived with the correct windows.

The window company never apologized; they never offered any compensation for the customer's troubles, which included four days off from work to wait for installation and "repair" crews. And he never did hear from that salesperson again.

The result was a high-priced purchase that inevitably left the customer with buyer's remorse, even with a high-quality product.

This customer will definitely never be a brand advocate for the company and in fact has told many friends about his negative experience.

Now let's compare that experience to the one a customer had buying a car. He carefully researched makes and models in the "premium" category and finally decided on an entry-level BMW that had won best-in-class awards from a number of automotive magazines.

After test driving the car, the customer felt that the company's motto, "the Ultimate Driving Machine," was perfectly accurate.

Like the window customer, this customer had a good experience with his salesperson.

Not only was the sales process easy, but the salesperson answered all of his questions and even sat with him to demonstrate all of the car's features. He also called a few days later to make sure the customer was enjoying his new car and to see if he had thought of any new questions.

When it came time for the customer's first service appointment, he was pleasantly surprised.

The service associate was friendly and once again answered all of his questions. He was pleased to hear that all of the work being done was covered by his bumper-to-bumper warranty and that he would be receiving brand-new wiper blades even before they were due to be replaced.

He was even more pleased when he entered the waiting room to see plenty of comfortable seating, free Wi-Fi, a full-time chef preparing made-to-order omelets and egg sandwiches for breakfast, and unlimited coffee, juice, bottled water, and sodas.

Although he had to wait about ninety minutes for the work on his car to be completed, he barely noticed the wait because he was eating a delicious breakfast and catching up on work emails on his laptop.

When it was time to retrieve his car, the service associate let him know they had also washed the car at no charge.

This customer remains loyal to BMW and is sure that when it comes time to replace his car, he will do so with another BMW.

Some interesting parallels arise between these two customers: They both spent about the same amount of money on their purchase, and they both had good sales experiences.

But for one, the positive feelings associated with the new purchase evaporated quickly when the "repair team" and customer service failed him. For the other, the positive sales experience was reinforced several times during the service experience.

The result? One is a happy BMW customer for life (and will likely upgrade to a more expensive model in the future), while the other is writing negative Yelp reviews and telling all of his friends never to buy windows from that national company. One is a brand advocate, and the other is a brand detractor.

So what can companies do to be more like BMW instead of the window company?

- Align sales with both marketing and customer service. Ensure that what marketing is promising matches what sales is selling and that customer service is ready to reliably help out if something goes wrong.

- Teach salespeople that the sale doesn't end when the commission check clears. Sales staff should take responsibility for ensuring a flawless installation or delivery and should check back early and often with a new customer to ensure his or her satisfaction.

- If something goes wrong with a new customer, the salesperson should not delegate the job to a "repair team" or customer service. They should take personal ownership of the problem and figure out how to fix it.

Teach the entire organization that the customer experience is what drives future sales. The window company may have sold one set of windows, but that's just a single transaction. BMW, on the other hand, is likely to make one or more additional automobile sales from that customer and his friends because they have continued to treat him like a valued customer.

☆ ☆ ☆ ☆ ☆

To avoid turning a handoff or transition into a customer pain point, ensure that each employee who is responsible for a certain part of the customer journey is also responsible for knowing where the customer came from and where they are going next.

Even if the company is siloed, the teams before and after a specific journey experience should be informed of any changes or improvements, and employees should always walk through the entire journey as if they were customers.

Remember, the customer doesn't care about your company's organizational structure. The fact that one team is responsible for acquisition, another is responsible for service, and a third for the digital experience *is not the customer's problem.* To them, it's all a single experience.

Best-in-class companies either operate more efficiently without silos or successfully hide the silos from the customer.

Chapter 12

DESIGNING THE RIGHT DIGITAL EXPERIENCE

Nilay Patel, editor-in-chief of *The Verge*, wrote a great column in advance of the popular Consumer Electronics Show (CES) in 2018. The headline read: "Everything is too complicated."[105]

Patel noted that while CES was always fun because it unveiled brand-new gadgets to the world, he wasn't sure if the world was ready.

"Most people have no idea how any of these things work, and are already hopelessly confused by the tech they have," he wrote. "The tech industry is starting to make these assumptions faster than anyone can reasonably be expected to keep up."[106]

After an informal survey of friends and family, Patel learned that many people were confused about the difference between Wi-Fi and Bluetooth, why some text messages are green while others are blue, whether Hulu and Roku are the same thing, and more. These are things that appear basic but only because those of us "in the know" assume everyone else is.

Former Chicago Cubs manager Joe Maddon coined the mantra "Do Simple Better" to ensure that the basics are never forgotten.

In baseball, Maddon is talking about always making the routine plays, whether it's fielding a ground ball, sliding into second, or laying down a bunt. In business, this equates to making every interaction with the customer easier.

Simplicity is a basic tenet of customer experience, but it is often overlooked in favor of a company's outdated rules or procedures.

Doing simple better means aiming for the fewest clicks (or taps) possible to complete a digital task, allowing a customer to easily talk to a human being on the phone if they need to, and writing legal terms and conditions in language customers can understand.

The mantra can be broken down into three parts from a digital perspective: reducing customer effort, using clear language, and providing easy navigation.

Reducing Customer Effort

Reducing customer effort, as we learned earlier from the *Harvard Business Review*, is the single most important factor in gaining customer loyalty.

Then why, as Patel notes, is everything "too complicated?"

Often things that make sense "on paper" don't translate correctly to "real life." The best way to suss out these potential customer pain points? Go through the entire journey and try to "break things."

Digital design is about making things people use; think of it conceptually not as a website or mobile app but as an experience.

Completing tasks on your digital properties, whether it's your website, mobile app, or social media page, should require low effort from users.

Case Study: Ordering Flowers via Chatbot

A client asked me to talk about a great chatbot experience, so I started doing some research. Using a chatbot, I ordered flowers from a well-known national company that none other than Facebook founder and CEO Mark Zuckerberg had lauded for its Facebook Messenger experience.

The ordering part was great. I got to view a bunch of arrangements, select the one I wanted, and see the pricing. It was more or less like the chatbot holding my hand through the ordering process on the website.

Then after I selected "The Delightful Daffodil" bouquet, it gave me three date options on which they could be delivered. Unfortunately, I wanted none of the dates.

I couldn't figure out what to do, so I typed "Help" into the chat. The bot figured that out and replied with, "What are you looking to do? Start over? Keep going? Or talk to support?"

I typed, "Talk to support." Then the bot responded with, "Customer service is closed."

That left me wondering: *Why did it offer me the choice of talking to support in the first place?*

Then it really got weird. Right after learning that customer service was closed, I got another response from "Samantha": "Hey, Dan. I'm Samantha, a live agent. How may I help you?"

Now I was really confused. So I wrote to Samantha, "Hey, I was just experimenting. I haven't used a bot before. Nothing specific, but thanks for the help." At this point the bot replied, "What would you like to change?" and gave me three options. Then Samantha also replied: "Okay, Dan. Feel free to reach out to us if you'd like any assistance."

Suddenly, I was talking with the bot and Samantha at the same time.

It started off as a pretty easy interaction—I wanted to order flowers, which is a basic task. There are only so many choices, and building a bot around that is pretty simple. But when I ran into trouble with the date and I needed to talk to a human, the whole experience fell apart.

The lesson: A bot is supposed to enhance the experience, not destroy it. Bots must be programmed to bring in a human at the very second they can't solve the problem, and, of course, the human should then override the bot.

☆ ☆ ☆ ☆ ☆

See how the flower example qualifies as "Everything is too complicated" instead of "doing simple better"?

When designing for simplicity in digital, guard against what's called "choice overload."

"The phenomenon of choice overload occurs as a result of too many choices being available to consumers," according to BehavioralEconomics.com. "Overchoice has been associated with unhappiness, decision fatigue, going with the default option, as well as choice deferral—avoiding making a decision altogether, such as not buying a product."[107]

In other words, reducing the number of choices and simplifying the options can be helpful to your customers and potential customers and also get them to buy more.

Sometimes, no choice is required at all.

When attempting to deposit a check through my bank's mobile app, the app asks where I want the funds placed.

The only problem is that *I only have one account.*

So why does the app give me this "choice" every single time?

Clearly the functionality was built for customers who have more than one account, but the developers forgot about the percentage of customers that only have a single account.

The best digital experiences don't get in the user's way and just let them do their thing on their own terms. Helping them accomplish their task by eliminating roadblocks will also reduce frustration and improve satisfaction.

In fact, 82 percent of customers say technology should make their online experiences with brands better.[108]

Is your online experience delivering on that promise?

Using Clear Language

Are Americans illiterate when it comes to healthcare? According to a consumer survey by Policygenius,[109] the answer is yes. But are the consumers to blame, or is the healthcare industry itself?

Policygenius surveyed 2,000 Americans and asked them a seemingly simple question: Can you define four basic health insurance terms? The four terms were: deductible, coinsurance, co-pay and out-of-pocket maximum.

A healthy 83 percent of respondents were confident that they "definitely understand" what a co-pay is, maybe because they have to physically reach in their wallet and hand money to a receptionist. This compared to 74 percent who were confident that they "definitely understand" what a deductible is; 67 percent who said they knew what out-of-pocket maximum means; and just 47 percent who claimed to understand coinsurance.

But here's the rub: The percentage of people who could actually recite the correct definition was just 52 percent for co-pay, 50 percent for deductible, 42 percent for out-of-pocket maximum, and 22 percent for coinsurance.

Worse, only 4 percent of Americans could correctly define all four terms.

What's remarkable is that these are not uncommon terms. In fact, they represent some of the main functioning aspects of any health insurance plan.

Consumers were likely confident about the words because they recognize them from the inappropriately named document called the "Explanation of Benefits"—inappropriate because it rarely provides a satisfactory explanation, and it is often not beneficial.

The industry gibberish doesn't stop there, with lists of drugs being called "formularies" and Medicare having Parts A, B, and D but not C.

Terms like "out-of-pocket maximum" are almost intentionally misleading; it sounds like the amount of money a patient has to reach into his or her pocket for to pay for healthcare, but that definition contains a major asterisk (lawyer-speak for "but there's fine print.")

That definition is right, asterisk, as long as the doctors that you are visiting are always in your network. If you go out of network, asterisk, your "out-of-pocket maximum" is usually much higher and the in-network and out-of-network amounts are not combined.

Confused yet?

Even more remarkable than the existence of all these confusing terms, though, is that the Policygenius survey is several years old and healthcare companies are still using the same language—even though they know consumers don't understand it.

As is the case with many facets of the customer experience in healthcare, lawyers and regulators often shoulder the blame. But is this fair?

Yes, regulations are lengthy and confusing, and their required language often uses the same confusing industry jargon. And well-intentioned legislation mandates so much of the solution, leaving marketers and customer experience professionals without much leeway for innovation.

But companies also hide behind legislation, with answers like "Well, legally we have to do it."

Even if laws required insurance companies to use the word "coinsurance," which only 22 percent of Americans understand, how hard would it be for them to define that term for the customer?

Some companies have figured out how to turn legal disclosure into an experience.

For example, instead of starting a paragraph of legalese with the word "Disclaimer," they might say something like, "A Word from Our Lawyers" and then try to "translate" the legalese into plain English.

Network Health Wisconsin uses simple language as its competitive advantage.

In its Twitter profile, the company notes: "Health insurance causes people stress. That's beyond ironic. Network Health is determined to fix that."

And on a section of its website entitled, "We Speak Your Language," Network Health Wisconsin says that "When you call Network Health, you won't be overwhelmed by health insurance language. We talk like people, not insurance dictionaries."

This phenomenon isn't limited to the healthcare industry.

Companies in all industries should look at their own contracts and other legal documents to see if the language can be simplified so it is more likely to be understood. Is it something that is so clear that an eighth grader could read and understand what is being expected, what is being promised, and what is going to be delivered?

What are the jargon words in your industry? Every industry has them. They might be difficult, archaic, hard-to-understand words. They might be acronyms that everyone in your office building knows but no customer knows.

If you can, stop using these words and start using words that your customers understand. If not, make sure you find a way to translate these words into plain English for your customers. When your customers understand what you're trying to communicate, you're both achieving the initial goal of the legalese—communicating important information—and building trust with your customers because you're speaking their language.

The daughter of a Forrester researcher received an email from a major bank with an offer she simply didn't understand: *Earn 0% APY with an IRA CD.*

"Is this even English??? Someone explain what this means," she wrote to her father, Forrester VP Dipanjan Chatterjee.

The email subject line, containing only eight words, had three acronyms in it, all financial services industry terms that are not widely understood by the general public.

Chatterjee shared the interaction and his thoughts on his LinkedIn profile.

"That's my daughter's reaction after being messaged by her bank. She is old enough to be somewhat curious, but young enough to be utterly befuddled," he wrote. "The financial services category is in dire need of a lesson in communication relevance. Often providing a better brand experience doesn't take a lot of money, tech, or people. It takes common sense."

With many large companies, including banks, dedicating entire departments to customer experience and focused on improving interactions throughout the customer journey, how can a marketing campaign like this pass muster, especially with a target audience of young professionals?

Even seasoned banking customers may have difficulty defining APY (annual percentage yield), which is different from the more typical APR (annual percentage rate).[110] Combining APY with two other acronyms makes the advertisement unnecessarily confusing.

In every industry, companies use internal jargon. But this jargon often leaks into marketing with the belief that customers speak the same language.

So the answer to Chatterjee's daughter's question "Is this even English???" is no, it's not. It's a language called Bank, one of many industry languages spoken only by industry insiders.

Case Study: Language Analysis

A report by VisibleThread, a content and language analytics company, looked at the top fifty banks in the US and their communications, finding that 58 percent of US bank content is not readable for the average American.

Confirming that readability is an industrywide issue in financial services, VisibleThread also found that even the best ten bank websites are harder to read than *Moby Dick*.[111] Likewise, a separate study found that two-thirds of US health insurers produce content more difficult to read than the same literary classic.[112]

That's right, it is easier to read a seminal piece of English literature that was written in 1851 than it is to read content from a top bank or health insurer.

The insurance report found that 86.6 percent of insurers are not communicating effectively with the target audience for Medicare, age sixty-five or older.

"Health insurance companies who communicate clearly create a higher level of trust," the report stated. "Trusted brands attract new customers and maintain their existing base."[113]

The bank report identified "jargon-laden, complex language," "academic tone of voice," and "long sentences" as the main drags on readability scores, with only one out of fifty banks scoring at an acceptable average sentence length and nearly 90 percent using passive voice at excessive levels.

VisibleThread placed banks alongside other writings in a scoring system based on the premise that the average American reads at the eighth-grade level. A readability score of fifty or higher, according to the company, will achieve optimal reach and comprehension.

For comparison, the *Harvard Law Review* scored a 30, whereas the *Harry Potter* books scored a 72.8. *Moby Dick* came in at 57.9, and an academic research paper on chess scored a 40.

The top-scoring ten banks landed at exactly 50. The next thirty banks scored 48.4, and the bottom ten banks scored 40.5.

So the worst ten banks communicate at a readability level that is comparable to an academic paper on chess.[114]

Readability goes beyond marketing materials. It includes legal terms and conditions, signage, and the website and mobile app.

But marketing, it would seem, should be among the easiest communications to read because it's aimed at getting people to take action.

"Culture can create a preconception that regulations and compliance matters must be complex," according to VisibleThread. "And because they are highly educated, industry employees overestimate the average customer's sophistication."[115]

For example, VisibleThread took a complex legal disclosure and simplified it as follows:

Original Copy: "The exact fee will be disclosed when the promotional offer is made to you, and will be charged when the transaction is posted to your account." This sentence has twenty-six words, four instances of passive voice, and an 11.8 grade level.

Suggested Copy: "When we give you the promotional offer, we'll let you know the exact fee. And we will charge you when we post the transaction to your account." This is two simpler sentences, no instances of passive voice, and a 4.8 grade level.[116]

So what can companies in any industry do to improve readability scores? VisibleThread offers these four simple changes:

- Reduce sentence length
- Eliminate passive voice
- Choose less complex words
- Adopt technology to help[117]

In addition, these four tactics will help your company think differently about language:

1. Read customer communications out loud, just like your high school English teacher used to tell you to do. This will help you "hear" the words as a customer would.

2. Simplify all communications used for customers by reducing the reliance on industry jargon and acronyms.

3. Test your communications—especially marketing—with sample audiences before rolling out a campaign to ensure that the offer (and accompanying terms) are well understood. Otherwise you may be wasting valuable marketing dollars.

4. Ask some eighth graders to read and explain the communications. If they can't, it's likely your customers won't be able to either. Don't know any eighth graders? Ask an employee to take the communications home to their kid to review.

"Companies who communicate clearly create a higher level of trust," notes VisibleThread. "Trusted brands attract new customers and maintain their existing base."[118]

☆ ☆ ☆ ☆ ☆

Providing Easy Navigation

Perhaps the most important factor regarding the perceived simplicity (or lack thereof) of a digital experience is the navigation.

How important are those navigation labels at the top of your website?

According to research conducted by branding, design, and marketing agency Tank Design, labels are essential—as long as you care about your customers finding what they're looking for.

After all, it's not called "navigation" for nothing.

But many large companies, especially in the B2B space, use the *exact same* navigation labels on their websites, leading to no differentiation for either potential customers or the omnipresent overseer of website usability, Google.

It turns out that people generally don't know what's hiding behind generic labels like "Products," "Solutions," "Services," and "Resources" because they all sound interchangeable.

"We were seeing a pattern that became undeniable," said Tank's senior user experience designer Hilary Basch, who along with senior manager of data insights and analytics Laurel Marcus, conducted an in-depth survey of what site users think certain navigations mean. "We were having such a hard time convincing our clients to move away from it because so many people were doing it."[119]

Basch and Marcus believed that a better user experience was possible. User experience, or UX, is an important subset of customer experience.

According to the International Organization for Standardization, user experience is a "user's perceptions and responses that result from the use and/or anticipated use of a system, product or service" and is "a consequence of brand image, presentation, functionality, system performance, interactive behaviour and assistive capabilities of a system, product or service."[120]

The Tank Design team decided to conduct its own research after failing to find concrete evidence of what they had always assumed.

"While there was research out there explaining the danger of vague labels, we couldn't find hard evidence to convince clients that these 'marketing terms' didn't resonate with users and had a potential for real impact on the experience, engagement, and even conversion," Basch said. "Our hypothesis is that terms hold meaning for those behind the curtain, but we proved that they don't for users."

The researchers developed a realistic scenario of a small business owner searching for a conference call solution that works across multiple countries. They then asked 217 respondents to imagine that they went to a company's website and encountered a fairly typical navigation strip containing five options: Features, Platform, Products, Services, and Solutions.

"After we set the scene, we asked participants to make their best guess about where specific content would be," Basch explained. "For example, where would you find information on international call rates? Integrations? Mobile capabilities?" There were five such location questions.

Across all demographics, including gender, geography, income, age, and education, the results were the same: "What we found is that no matter how you sliced the results, there was no consensus," said Basch.

"Consensus" was defined ahead of time as 75 percent of users picking the same location for a certain piece of content—a fairly low bar because it still means one in four users would fail to find the correct spot.

Of the five questions, only one even saw more than 50 percent of users choosing the same label, and in every question, at least 5 percent chose every single label. In other words, total digital chaos.

"That's a failure," said Basch. Failure, indeed.

According to separate research by famed website usability expert Jakob Nielsen of Nielsen Norman Group, the average webpage visit lasts less than a minute, and to increase that, companies "must clearly communicate your value proposition within 10 seconds."[121]

"That's not enough time to tolerate failure," Basch cautioned.

So what's the answer?

"Labels should be as specific and clear as possible," said Basch. Tank cites Chewy.com as a good example; after choosing "Shop by Pet," the site presents users with clear, descriptive labels: Food, Treats, Supplies.

Specific labels have the added benefit of helping not just user experience but also search engine optimization (SEO). "Being specific in your navigation encourages Google to route searches to your website," Basch said.

Companies should choose navigation labels that make sense from a user's perspective, even if they aren't the exact same terminology used internally.

"Let your customers tell you how you should be organizing your offering," Basch advised. "They often can say it better than you can because they're not mired in how it all works behind the scenes."

Companies that don't heed this advice and instead insist on looking like everyone else will face consequences.

"By using vague navigation labels, we've proven that you are creating space for failure and missing an opportunity to create clarity around your brand and offering," Basch said. "If [users] are failing to find the content they're looking for, they will go to your competitors or somewhere else."

Navigation doesn't just apply to websites. At a local gas station, drivers can redeem rewards earned at the grocery store for discounts on gas. The only problem? Redeeming that reward can be a little tricky.

Imagine you drive up to the gas station, get out of the car, and walk over to the fuel pump. The screen says "Swipe Easy Rewards or Easy Pay card now," except you don't have an Easy Rewards or Easy Pay card nor do you know what those are.

Then you see three choices associated with buttons next to the screen: Credit, Debit, and Rewards. You choose Rewards because you want to redeem your grocery points.

The next screen says "Select Reward," and again, you face three button choices: Rewards, Jewel ID/FR, and Cancel. You're pretty sure that "Cancel" isn't right, but you just chose "Rewards" on the last screen so that one is a bit confusing. Unfortunately, you don't know what a "Jewel ID/FR" is either, although Jewel is the name of the grocery store. Feeling a bit like Indiana Jones in *The Last Crusade*, you choose Rewards again.

You chose . . . wisely.

The top of the next screen says "Insert Rewards Card" even though you've already noted that you don't have a rewards card. Thankfully, yet another three button choices await you: Alt ID, Manual Entry/Barcode, and Cancel.

Is this even English?

I'll spare you the trouble because I spent way too much time going down every option path to figure this out. Guess what an "Alt ID" is?

It's simply your phone number.

Why couldn't the opening screen just have said "Enter your phone number"? It would have saved so many steps and so much frustration.

Phrases like "Easy Rewards or Easy Pay card," "Jewel ID/FR," "Alt ID," and "Manual Entry/Barcode" may mean something to company employees and programmers, but they don't mean anything to customers.

Another way to get customers' attention with a digital experience: Personalize it. People often credit the famous writer Dale Carnegie with saying, "Remember that a person's name is to that person the sweetest and most important sound in any language."[122]

As it turns out, Carnegie's observation works in digital formats too—and not just websites and mobile apps.

When customers arrive at the Fields BMW dealership in Northfield, Illinois, for a service appointment, they enter the garage by driving over what looks like a speed bump. This unassuming bump serves two purposes.

First, it reads the tires and instantly produces a report that shows each tire's pressure and tread wear, with images included. A technician shows the customer the report as soon as he or she exits the vehicle.

Second, the reduced speed while going over the bump allows for a quick scan of the front license plate. This action instantly leads to a personalized welcome message displayed on a screen right above where the customer parks the car in the garage.

The sign reads: "Welcome Back Guest" with the customer's name in all caps.

This is a great example of a simple customer experience improvement that is both personalized and Shareable. Not surprisingly, many customers snap a photo of the sign to post on social media.

The dealership had to invest in the scanner and the TV screen, but this one-time investment positively affects every experience of every person driving in after that. If you don't have the budget for such an investment, you could still welcome clients or visitors to your office with a simple PowerPoint slide on a screen.

The experience works because it's personal. Personalizing an experience by using a customer's name is an easy tactic that most businesses skip even though they already have their customers' names available in a database.

It feels nice to see your name up in lights on a screen. It's unique and memorable, and it's not something you see when you walk into most retail locations. It could be done on almost any website where the customer has previously placed an order or logged in.

The takeaway? Using somebody's name is a little thing, and it's not that hard to do. Every business can do it. Little things matter, and they can affect the experience in a big way.

When designing for digital, start with customer needs. If you don't know them, then ask; customers usually aren't shy about sharing opinions.

Use prototypes to get early validation and usability testing to confirm ease of use.

Be iterative: Release updates early and often, always demonstrating new value. As one design agency once told me, spend as much time iterating the problem as the solution.

Finally, never underestimate the importance of the digital experience.

According to Acquia, 63 percent of customers say they "often abandon a brand for another when the online experience is poor." And 72 percent say they are "loyal to certain brands, but as soon as I have a bad experience with them, I move on."[123]

Chapter 13

ADAPTING TO CHANGING TRENDS IN THE CONTACT CENTER

W hy is the contact center so important? Remember the quote from Chris Zane, founder and CEO of Zane's Cycles: "Customer service starts when the customer experience fails."[124]

It would be great if your company didn't need a customer service team, but eventually something will go wrong with your product or service. What happens next can mean the difference between a loyal customer and a lost one.

"Loyalty is tied to a customer's ongoing choice to do business with you, refer others to you, give you the benefit of the doubt, and have the sense of a positive relationship with you. Or the alternative: cut ties and take their business to your competitor," noted a report by Zendesk. "The factor that determines which door your customers choose is service: good experiences drive loyalty. Bad experiences tank it."[125]

When the company asked consumers which are the most frustrating aspects of a bad customer service experience, more than half said long hold or wait times while interacting with an agent. About 40 percent said either automated systems that make it hard to reach a human agent or having to repeat information multiple times.

In terms of the most important aspects of a good customer service experience, 60 percent said it occurs when an issue is resolved quickly, and more than 40 percent said it happens when support is available 24/7.[126]

The key trends that contact centers need to pay attention to are hiring, speed and consistency, self-service, and chatbots.

Hiring

In the past, a contact center hired just a couple of demographics to fill customer service agent roles, and those agents had to be good at one thing: solving problems on the telephone.

Today, with people working longer and the oldest members of Generation Z having graduated college, some contact centers have *five* generations of employees handling telephone, email, live chat, social media, and private messaging.

Each of the five generations—the Silent Generation, Baby Boomers, Generation X, Generation Y, and Generation Z—prefers different methods of communication, has different attitudes toward technology, chooses different customer service channels as consumers, and is focused on different career goals.

To develop the most productive workforce, contact centers must be cognizant of different types of employees and their needs. These needs may include work schedules, work from home versus in person, dress code, subject matter expertise, familiarity with certain customer service channels, and more.

Mentoring and "reverse-mentoring" programs can also help build skill sets across generations and make everyone feel like they have something to contribute.

In addition to the human element, multiple social media platforms (Facebook, Twitter, Instagram, etc.) and multiple messaging services (Facebook Messenger, Twitter direct message, WhatsApp, WeChat, etc.) exist from which customers can communicate. In recent years, this has made things a whole lot more complicated in the contact center.

Writing has also become a key skill set for a role that required barely any of it a couple of decades ago. In fact, the majority of customer service interactions today, including on all digital channels, are done in writing.

Today's customer service agents must be able to write well, with proper spelling and grammar, because their responses to customers reflect the brand. Further, in the public realm of social media, typographical errors and grammar mistakes can be costly from a public relations perspective.

Speed and Consistency

Speed and consistent service delivery across channels are key success factors for contact centers today.

The need for speed has evolved since the advent of social media and "real-time" conversations.

"Customers want fast replies to their questions, on the channel of their choice," according to Zendesk. "They choose channels based on the speed of reply they want and around the complexity of their question."[127]

According to a study by Medallia and Ipsos, "Today's consumers expect to engage in real-time dialogue with companies across touchpoints to get what they need without delay," and 70 percent of consumers say they expect an immediate response when they submit a complaint.[128]

The consistency issue often shows up in social media, where agents can be more empowered than their counterparts in other channels to make problems go away so customers won't complain publicly.

The result is many stories like this one that a friend of mine posted on social media (naturally):

> *I booked a flight a month ago for the wrong day and realized my error yesterday . . . I called [the airline] last night to tell my story and they told me if I wanted to switch flights it would cost me $100 and 15,000 miles . . . I was on the phone for about 30 minutes.*

He then shared a screenshot of his private message chat with the airline on Twitter:

> *Friend: My flight was booked for the wrong day. Need to be at ORD on 4/5, not 4/6. Any way you can help out? Confirmation #[redacted]. Thanks in adv!*
>
> *Airline: You're all set. An email is on the way with the correct return date. ^JJ*
>
> *Friend: JJ - you are a hero! Thank you so much and have a terrific day!*

That entire transaction took less time than the thirty minutes my friend had spent on the telephone.

What's the problem with this engagement? The airline has taught my friend to come only to social media to get what he wants, when he should have received the same treatment and resolution in any service channel.

The Medallia and Ipsos study found that 56 percent of online retail shoppers and 49 percent of offline shoppers expect consistent levels of service across physical and digital channels.

"Regardless of when, how, or why they are interacting with your brand, customers expect the experience to be seamless and efficient," the report stated.[129]

To avoid inadvertently creating an inconsistent experience for your customers, ensure that all contact center employees, regardless of channel, receive the same policy training and are empowered equally to solve customer problems.

Self-Service

Another important trend in the contact center is the continued move to self-service.

According to American Express, more than 60 percent of US consumers say their go-to channel for simple inquiries is a digital self-service tool (such as a website, mobile app, voice response system, or online chat).[130]

Despite that data, Zendesk found that "self-service is a missed opportunity" because "only a third of companies offer some form of self-service, whether through a help center, knowledge base, or FAQ."[131]

Self-service options provide a mutually beneficial solution to the customer and the company. For the customer, it saves time and effort (remember that reducing customer effort is the most important factor in customer loyalty). For the company, it saves the cost of handing additional customer service interactions for the same issue.

According to Zendesk, 69 percent of customers want to resolve as many issues as possible on their own, and 63 percent of customers always or almost always start with a search on a company's online resources when they have an issue.[132]

Lori Brown, chief marketing officer of The Results Companies, a leading business process outsourcing (BPO) company, noted that "we are devoted to technology and innovation, and recently our innovation division came up with something [that was] almost counterintuitive for a BPO. In short, our team came up with an opportunity to offer products that facilitate the rapid deployment of self-service out to everyone out there."[133]

Why might self-service be considered "counterintuitive" for Brown's company? Because they supply the human capital that fills contact centers, so theoretically self-service options would give them *less* work to do.

But The Results Companies understands the benefits of self-service and creates a loyal client base by recommending the best solutions even if it might mean less revenue for themselves.

"We are a people business, and that is what we do," Brown said. "But we also recognize that innovation is needed here, and being able to help out is what we really are striving to do."

She added that "the innovation that comes from a self-service perspective has left BPOs with more calls for concerns of the complex type. Therefore, if you think about it, it elevates the skill level that we need, and subsequently, the training that we have to supply to our agents.[134]

Chatbots

It probably comes as no surprise that when this customer experience enthusiast passed by a big sign in San Francisco that said, "Robotic Coffeebar," he had to check it out.

When you walk into this coffee shop, right away you notice there's actually nobody else in there, at least not at two in the afternoon. There are no humans. It is just a bunch of digital menu boards and some kiosks and this big robot in the back that is protected by glass. The robot is basically a long arm like you might find in a factory, and you can tell that there's some coffee-making machinery behind the glass with it.

The menu contains almost everything you might find at a bigger coffee shop, including (since it's San Francisco) many types of alternative milk products. The touchscreen kiosks walk the customer through the ordering and payment process and present an order number.

At this point, the robot starts to do its thing, working the coffee machines like a human barista. It makes a coffee and puts it down behind the glass on a counter. When the customer approaches the robot and enters the order number, the robotic arm again springs to life, grabs the coffee it previously set down, and puts it in what can only be described as a little coffee elevator where the cup then descends to a landing spot where the customer can pick it up.

The result, in my case, was a hot, steaming latte that looked and tasted really good.

Interestingly, the coffee is delivered without a lid (the customer puts it on themselves) so the artistry of the foam design is visible, something that has gotten lost in the to-go world of coffee.

CafeX operated several retail locations and also some "pop-ups" on busy street corners, where dozens of people could be seen taking pictures and videos of the robotic barista in action.

I found the CafeX experience to be fascinating, fun, fast, and convenient. It's probably not something I would do every day, but I would definitely tell my friends about it and probably invite them to experience it for themselves.

It turns out that CafeX was not alone in testing robots for food and beverages in San Francisco.

"The tech-centric city has seen an automized restaurant scene in recent years," Business Insider reported. "The idea is that robots could be used to fill repetition-heavy positions that require hours of nonstop work—like line cooking—that could then free up human employees to provide higher quality customer service. Labor costs and, subsequently, menu prices would be lowered, tipping would become obsolete, restaurants could more heavily invest in higher quality ingredients, and profits would increase for business owners in the process—or at least that's the theory."[135]

In any discussion about robots—"bots" for short—the inevitable question arises: Will robots take over the world and everyone's jobs with it?

Alas, the CafeX experiment mostly failed, as the company closed all of its San Francisco locations except for two airport spots. Other robot-inspired restaurants have met the same fate.

From Business Insider: "There could be multiple reasons why some of them have flopped, but perhaps a straightforward explanation is that we're simply not ready to be served by robots in lieu of humans."[136]

An airport location seems more conducive to a robotic coffee bar because of customers' state of mind: Just give me my coffee so I can run to the plane. Compare that to a coffee shop, where companies like Starbucks have established an atmosphere of human interaction and "lingering" that has become commonplace.

Robot-run food and beverage establishments are reminiscent of the explosive growth of automated teller machines (ATMs) at banks in the 1980s.

The ATM was the perfect solution for the simple banking transaction of withdrawing money from an account. It didn't remove human tellers from the equation; it just freed them up to handle the more complex transactions like account openings and loans.

In other words, sometimes technology for technology's sake doesn't make an impact, but using technology to augment the customer experience can be a game-changer for both the company and the customer.

That brings us to the topic of chatbots in a contact center. What exactly is a chatbot?

"At the most basic level, a chatbot is a computer program that simulates and processes human conversation (either written or spoken), allowing humans to interact with digital devices as if they were communicating with a real person," according to Oracle. "Chatbots can be as simple as rudimentary programs that answer a simple query with a single-line response, or as sophisticated as digital assistants that learn and evolve to deliver increasing levels of personalization as they gather and process information."[137]

The technology associated with chatbots is called artificial intelligence, or AI, which is just what it sounds like: Nonhumans (computers) demonstrating some form of "intelligent" thought. Often, AI is used to have computers sort and tabulate mountains of data in a fraction of the time it would take a human to perform the same task. In the case of chatbots, the computer is identifying words in a conversation, processing what they mean, and offering a response.

Effective chatbots can provide answers to routine or repetitive questions, allowing customer service agents to work on more difficult cases. Think of these questions as anything the customer probably could have Googled. You can also use them to guide the customer through a standard process, like ordering flowers, as in the earlier example.

A big benefit of chatbots: They can be built once and then deployed across many platforms, including Facebook Messenger, Twitter, a website, Skype, WeChat, WhatsApp, Kik, Line, Viber, and more.

Chatbots should not be used as a digital IVR, or interactive voice response system (think "Press 1 for your balance, Press 2 to pay your bill . . .") because we already know these systems annoy and frustrate customers on the phone, so there is no sense in replicating that negative interaction digitally.

When combined with machine learning (ML), bots can "learn" over time, improving their performance and even personalizing interactions.

Like with coffee and ATMs, the success or failure of a chatbot will depend on customers' willingness to use them.

According to Acquia, 75 percent of customers say the problem with automated experiences (interacting with technology instead of a real human) with a brand is that they are too impersonal.[138]

Chatbots can be incredibly valuable, however, when companies use them to help the human agent do a better job servicing the customer.

If you imagine a human agent sitting next to a supercomputer that's got every piece of data that they could ever want, instantly, it means that the agent can spend more time being human instead of clack, clack, clacking on their computer keyboard to find information. They can pay more attention to the conversation with the customer and be better at solving problems.

This may be why the robotic restaurants failed—because they attempted to remove the human interaction entirely from the experience, rather than integrating the robot interaction with the human one.

The best chatbots can answer lots of customer questions and know exactly when to bring in a human agent when the questions get too complex or if the customer requests it.

Chapter 14

SOLIDIFYING EXECUTIVE LEADERSHIP WITH A CHIEF EXPERIENCE OFFICER

A growing number of companies are installing a chief experience officer (CXO) into the C-suite, with responsibility for every facet of the customer journey. *Harvard Business Review* even makes the case that every company should have a CXO to oversee both customer experience and employee experience.[139]

A study by Zendesk found that "the factors that influence customer loyalty are owned across your sales, support, success, marketing, finance, and product organizations."

But when the company asked respondents, "Which leader owns the customer experience at your company?" the results were mixed:

- 35 percent said the chief customer officer
- 25 percent said the chief operating officer
- 12 percent said the chief experience officer
- 11 percent said the chief marketing officer
- 8 percent said the chief innovation officer
- 5 percent said some other executive role[140]

For the purposes of this discussion, we're going to consider a chief customer officer and a chief experience officer one and the same and use only the nomenclature of chief experience officer or CXO.

So what exactly is the job description for a CXO, and how do companies set such a role up for success?

According to *CEO Review,* "The scope of the CXO extends beyond a Customer Service Manager: as the spokesperson for the customer experience they are tasked with ensuring each aspect of the business contributes towards a positive engagement between the brand and the consumer."[141]

The publication further spells out five main objectives of the role:

1. Promote the culture of customer orientation internally
2. Develop knowledge and understanding of customers
3. Implement targeted campaigns to increase customer loyalty, retention, and satisfaction
4. Promote the customer perspective and make sure it is considered for all topics and projects of the organization
5. Measure all the factors that form the customer experience through various KPIs [Key Performance Indicators][142]

Kurt Schroeder is the CXO at Avtex Solutions, a leading full-service customer experience solution provider. He described his role as follows:

> *I wake up every morning and I think about, "How do we continually improve and deliver a better experience for our customers?"*
>
> *Why is that even important? I'm a firm believer that we live in a world where everything is about the experience. We live in the Experience Economy. . . .*
>
> *If you don't have someone who is thinking about that day-in, day-out, at night, when they're sleeping, when they're waking, when they're eating, then I think you're lagging behind. You're missing a great opportunity.*
>
> *So, what do I do when I get here in the morning? I think about, "What are the areas of our organization and the experience that we're rendering to our customers, that we really need to improve and make better and create differentiation in the market?"[143]*

Schroeder added that for a CXO to consider the entirety of the customer journey, he or she must focus on four facets: "find more customers, win more customers, keep more customers and do more for those customers."[144]

Previously, I introduced Tom Karinshak, the CXO at Comcast, a company that added chairs with the word "Customer" on them to executive offices and conference rooms as a constant reminder to remember the customer with every business decision.

"My job is to make sure that we put the customer at the center of everything that we go and do," Karinshak said in an interview, citing tactical implementations, strategic planning, systems, policies and processes as examples.[145]

Of equal importance, Karinshak added, is the employee experience.

"We can't have great customer experience without a great employee experience, or vice versa, and so we spend equal rigor on both sides of that equation," he said.

Many companies struggle with the question of whether customer experience should fall under a single department or whether it should be "everyone's job." Both methods have their challenges; a single department runs the risk of becoming an unwelcome intruder into everyone else's business (think auditors or government regulators), while making CX everyone's job can result in it actually being no one's job because it's no one's top priority.

In my corporate experience helping employees set goals, I found that unless a goal equated to a minimum of 20 percent of the annual evaluation, it usually didn't get done. So, if customer experience is less than 20 percent of anyone's goals, it probably won't be a priority.

At Comcast, a hybrid model of the two approaches has worked successfully.

"It's how people are held accountable from an overall performance perspective; it truly is everyone's job everywhere across the organization," Karinshak said. "But what we [the CX team] do is intensify the focus, set the strategy, support the coordination, make sure that there is alignment across all of the functions and all the channels so that it is a completely coordinated, aligned, coherent, consistent approach to the customer experience across the company."[146]

At Benco Dental, Larry Cohen, the patriarch of the family business, took on the role of "chief customer advocate" when he transitioned the day-to-day operations of the company to his two sons.

"It makes a big difference for the customers when they can get a Cohen on the phone, someone who's an owner, someone who can take their side and move mountains to get things done for customers," says Larry's son Chuck, managing director at Benco Dental. "He gets calls all the time. Sometimes he ends up yelling at people within the organization saying, 'How can we not take care of this customer?' Boy oh boy, that really gets people's attention. But having Larry as the chief customer advocate has been a terrific move for the organization and our customers."[147]

Chapter 15

COVID-19 AND THE FUTURE OF CUSTOMER EXPERIENCE

Everything changed for businesses in March 2020, with COVID-19 ravaging the economy, people's livelihoods, and, of course, their health.

Words and phrases like lockdown, quarantine, infection rate, stimulus bills, and even coin shortage entered the lexicon. Many companies shuttered their doors, and entire industries restructured and adapted to remain solvent, let alone competitive.

These were unprecedented times. Even the best crisis and business continuity plans were deemed worthless in a few short weeks. But a crisis is not the time to panic, especially when people are looking to businesses for confidence and guidance.

It is, in fact, the very best time to focus on customer experience and to show customers you are there for them.

And while we don't know what—or when—the next crisis will be, we can certainly be better prepared.

The good news for those of us focused on customer experience is that the pandemic brought CX to the forefront. Customers were depending on companies more than ever, and they were making future buying decisions based on their experience during the crisis.

"Customer experience has taken on a new definition and dimension in the overwhelming challenge of COVID-19," noted McKinsey. "Customer leaders who care and innovate during this crisis and anticipate how customers will change their habits will build stronger relationships that will endure well beyond the crisis' passing."[148]

In other words, customer experience became even more important during the pandemic, and the lessons taught in this book held true.

Some companies immediately understood the situation and pivoted to be more helpful and caring for their customers. Others kept plowing forward as if nothing had happened, occasionally checking a box by sending a copycat email talking about their enhanced cleaning procedures.

"Particularly in times of crisis, a customer's interaction with a company can trigger an immediate and lingering effect on his or her sense of trust and loyalty," wrote McKinsey. "As millions are furloughed and retreat into isolation, a primary barometer of their customer experience will be how the businesses they frequent and depend upon deliver experiences and service that meet their new needs with empathy, care and concern."[149]

Fear and anxiety were rampant among both customers and employees. As anxiety can negatively affect decision-making, you must think through business decisions thoroughly and discuss them with leadership before taking any decisive actions, including seemingly inconsequential things like social media posts.

When customers see businesses acting calmly and rationally, it helps them remain calm too.

Customer needs and expectations changed rapidly. After a brief respite where customers were sympathetic to companies trying to figure things out, the demand for support, convenience, and safety was even higher than before.

"Repeatedly, the businesses that have stayed ahead of the competition are those that have anticipated and met changing customer expectations," according to messaging platform Podium. "Those who take advantage of the moment and adapt will thrive and those who don't will lose their customers to those who do."[150]

A few key trends emerged that will remain meaningful for companies post-COVID-19 as well as in the face of any future crisis:

Preparation Is Key

Business continuity planning (BCP) is still a relatively new practice, but it's a good bet that every company will take it more seriously going forward. In fact, I predict that BCP experts will be in high demand for several years, as companies attempt to shore up risk and prepare for whatever lies ahead.

According to *Investopedia*, BCP "is the process involved in creating a system of prevention and recovery from potential threats to a company. The plan ensures that personnel and assets are protected and are able to function quickly in the event of a disaster . . . [and] involves defining any and all risks that can affect the company's operations."[151]

No longer can leaders sit in BCP meetings and scoff at hypothetical events that could "never happen." Trust me, I was in many of those meetings during my twenty years in Corporate America. We said that terrorist attacks could "never happen." We said the same thing about active shooter scenarios. We said it about hurricanes and tornadoes and earthquakes and tsunamis. We said it about cyber-attacks. And we definitely said it about pandemics.

No matter what business you're in, you have to be ready for something like COVID-19 to happen again. There is no longer any excuse to be unprepared.

Map out a detailed plan that anticipates the next crisis, using learnings from the last one. Hire an expert if you need to, as the entire fate of your business is at stake.

Manufacturers should consider how to immediately ramp up production or maintain certain quantities of inventory in case of emergency.

Corporations should be ready to have employees working from home instead of coming into the office at a moment's notice.

Grocery stores and restaurants should have plans in place to immediately move to curbside service if necessary.

Every company should consider a scenario in which it has to completely shut down for an undetermined amount of time.

All of these things eventually happened during COVID-19, but slowly and painfully. And the next crisis will not be exactly the same.

What does your business need to do to prepare for whatever crisis comes next? The time you spend now contemplating and planning out scenarios will help you, and your customers, down the line.

Focus on Safety

Safety has long been considered a core human need, and with rampant fears about the COVID-19 pandemic worldwide, safety once again returned to the forefront of people's minds. It will likely remain so for a long time, so you must consider it an important part of the customer experience going forward.

In 1943, American psychologist Abraham Maslow unveiled his now-famous hierarchy of needs, the psychological theory comprising a five-tier pyramid of human needs, ranked from physiological at the bottom (the most basic needs) to self-actualization at the top (the needs most difficult to attain).

"Safety needs," which include safety and security, are considered basic needs, ranked just above "physiological needs" such as food, water, warmth, and rest. Safety needs can also include physical safety, psychological safety, and emotional safety.

In the COVID-19 world, the need for safety stemmed from other emotions that countless people are feeling: stress, fear, loneliness, and even anger.

Psychology Today noted that five elements are commonly referred to as Psychological First Aid, often administered to victims of natural disasters but also applicable to a crisis like a pandemic.

Those five elements are:

1. Help people feel safe
2. Create a sense of calm
3. Help regain a sense of control and self-efficacy
4. Feed the need for social connection
5. Believe in the power of hope[152]

Grocery stores and pharmacies set the standard for processes and procedures that strive to ensure the safety of customers and employees.

The availability of hand sanitizer, limiting the number of patrons inside an establishment, requiring staff to wear personal protective equipment, installing plastic shields at checkouts, accepting contactless payments, and adopting directional signage resulting in a one-way traffic flow all became best practices.

Since customer experience incorporates every single interaction a customer has with a business, the strong psychological need for safety means that customers' perceptions of their safety (or lack thereof) will continue to play a large role in determining where they spend their hard-earned dollars.

According to Podium, 46 percent of customers say that "well-communicated safety practices and offering pick up/curbside/contactless services are in the top three most important factors in choosing a local business today."[153]

Connect with Customers

During the coronavirus pandemic, customers looked for calm and confidence. Since they were getting conflicting reports from the media and the government in many cases, they looked toward the businesses with which they had established a relationship.

The unique part about the pandemic of 2020? Virtually every person on the planet was going through the same thing at the same time. That made demonstrating empathy, long a core tenant of good customer experience strategy, more important than ever but also easier to achieve.

After all, if you couldn't show empathy when you knew exactly what your customers were going through, it's not likely that empathy will ever be a strong suit.

Martin Wilkinson-Brown, chief marketing officer at Sitel Group, wrote that the best companies address both the functional and emotional needs of their customers, especially during a crisis. In other words, you still have to resolve their business issues, but you can go a step further by treating them with a dose of humanity too.

"Simply asking customers how they are doing, or if there is anything the agent can do to help in this troubling time will go a long way toward putting customers at ease and creating a memorable experience," wrote Wilkinson-Brown. "By addressing the emotional needs of your customers during a crisis, you can help put them at ease and make them feel valued when they need it."[154]

Just checking in with customers and clients can make a powerful statement. In addition to mass emails, check in one-on-one with each customer if possible. A simple phone call, handwritten letter, or personal email can go a long way toward ensuring that your customers know you care about them on a human level, not just an economic one.

Remember that without customers, there is no business, so we should be doing everything we can to ensure our customers are still there when business returns to normal.

Millennials in particular want a human relationship with businesses, but this is extending to other generations as well. In many companies, entire teams weren't able to work their regular jobs for one reason or another; the smart companies gave these people something to do by connecting with customers.

"The first step in caring is to reach out—not in marketing or overt attempts to gain a competitive edge, but to offer genuine support," noted McKinsey.[155]

The middle of a crisis is the single most important time for companies to connect with their customers and cement long-term human relationships. As a former boss of mine liked to say, "Loyalty goes both ways."

In a time of crisis, we have to take the first step because our customers are depending on us.

So what are the best ways to communicate with customers during a crisis? The answer is the same as in "normal" times: Go where your customers are instead of making them come to you.

When customers call you, don't tell them to go to the website. When customers tweet at you, don't tell them to call. Rest assured that your customers know the available service channels; they are going to choose the channel they want, which isn't always going to be the channel you want, and that is OK.

It is the responsibility of the business to meet its customers where they are.

During COVID-19, when customers were stuck at home, texting became an even more important communication method.

Podium reported that more than 60 percent of consumers received or exchanged text messages with a local business during the early days of the pandemic.

"Now is the time to start messaging your customers—or risk losing them to businesses that do," noted Podium.[156]

One of the benefits of messaging: A company can be channel agnostic by employing a single messaging platform. In other words, customer service agents don't have to learn different messaging platforms like Facebook Messenger, WhatsApp, Twitter direct message, etc. (or even particularly care which one a customer is using) because all messages are consolidated into a single agent inbox.

Actions speak louder than words when it comes to connecting with customers during times of fear and uncertainty. Telling people "We are here for you" only goes so far; companies must show customers what "here for you" really means.

When they do, the connections they establish in the bad times will be remembered in the good times.

"By consciously providing empathy and care during this crisis, companies can build a foundation of goodwill and long-lasting emotional connections with the communities they serve," wrote McKinsey. "Leading in a caring, empathetic manner during these difficult times has the potential to create real connections that will outlive the social and economic impact of the pandemic."[157]

Take Care of Your Employees

It is a common customer experience mantra that happy employees equal happy customers, and like many things in the COVID-19 era, that feeling was exacerbated.

Unfortunately, the inverse is true too, so it is incumbent upon businesses to ensure that their employees feel healthy and safe and actually are healthy and safe.

Here are some tips to reach that goal:

- Always allow employees to prioritize taking care of their families first. (Incidentally, I've always told my employees that family comes first. Whether it's an illness or a lifecycle event, almost always the work can wait while we attend to the most important people in our lives.)
- Ensure that working conditions, whether in-person or at home, look and feel safe.
- Understand that working from home with kids (or pets) is a challenge, and workers are doing the best they can.
- Encourage employees to take wellness breaks during the day and to turn off their computers at night.

We can't expect employees to help customers feel safe if they don't feel safe themselves.

Just like with customers, it is critical to remain calm and exhibit confidence with employees as well. Employees look to company executives and their individual managers for guidance in times of uncertainty, so if you act calm and confident, they will too.

It's also OK to break from routine and have a little fun to ease the tension of working from home and the uncertainty of what's ahead. Consider these ideas to lighten up your next Zoom meeting:

- 💡 Encourage everyone to select a fun virtual background.
- 💡 Invite people to a toast with a glass of wine or a nonalcoholic drink.
- 💡 Have people share a funny moment or story.
- 💡 Schedule a crazy hat or ugly sweater day.
- 💡 Play a game together, like finding the most words among a set of letters on the screen.

One outcome of the COVID-19 pandemic: Many companies realized that working from home is doable. Traditional thinking said that workplace culture, face-to-face meetings, and a physical office building were all required to get work done; virtually every company in the world was forced into discovering that is not necessarily the case.

During the pandemic, one manager who works for a client of mine noted that she spent more time with her employees than at any point when they were all physically located in the same building.

Perhaps the strangest dynamic that resulted: Issues that typically led to firing off an email and waiting for a response were instead immediately resolved by jumping onto a Zoom call. The result was actually more "face time" than before the crisis kept everyone apart.

Employee experience is more in focus than ever before. Many workers report being busier during the day while working from home, foregoing lunch breaks, and skipping the daily commute. Of course, that presents a different issue, which is that employees need to find time to exercise, relax, or otherwise "turn off" work to maintain their sanity.

Then there's the juggling of kids, pets, and Wi-Fi bandwidth that everyone has to deal with, whether it's happening to you or someone else in your meeting.

One major appeal for companies is the potential to cut one of the biggest expense lines out of their budgets (besides employees): the cost of maintaining a physical building, which could include mortgage or rent, maintenance, utilities, security, cleaning services, equipment, supplies, insurance, and more.

Another advantage is the ability to extend hiring reach beyond the physical boundaries of an office, thereby opening up a much more diverse group of candidates for roles.

So with all that hassle and expense, why not just keep employees working from home? For some, it would be considered a huge perk, especially for people with kids and/or pets or a long commute. For others, however, missing out on the social aspects of an office and working in constant isolation may be too much to handle.

Whatever the case, employee safety will continue to be paramount because if employees don't feel safe, they can't make customers feel safe.

Understand Your Customers' Changing Needs

"In times of crisis, your customers will have new or enhanced concerns—and are likely to take new steps to obtain resolutions," wrote Avtex, a customer experience design and orchestration firm. "Take the time to chart out these new pathways and develop new strategies to support individual interactions and the overall customer journey. Doing so will help to limit pain points and reduce effort and frustration for all parties."[158]

Avtex further suggested that to reduce customer effort, companies should:

- Review each step involved in interactions
- Communicate often using multiple channels
- Think creatively

"During a crisis, supporting your customers and reducing their stress should be your focus. Explore every potential strategy for achieving that goal," the company concluded. "By reducing customer effort during a crisis, you can deliver experiences that your customers will truly appreciate and remember for years."[159]

Two good ways to stay connected with changing customer needs and expectations? Maintain consistent communication with them and your frontline employees who engage with them on a daily basis.

Changing needs of the customer, combined with state and local regulations and resource availability of companies, led to multiple customer experience enhancements that are likely to outlive the pandemic:

The Move to Digital

"The key coronavirus consumer trend is that increasingly a brand is judged by the strength of its digital channels when it comes to customer experience (CX)," wrote Martin Wilkinson-Brown, the chief marketing officer of Sitel Group.[160]

Their study found that as COVID-19 forced many physical stores to temporarily close and for the population to practice social distancing, consumers looked to digital channels to serve their needs.

Seventy-six percent of respondents said they'd made online purchases for things they normally would have purchased in-person, and, importantly, 57 percent said that they would continue with this behavior post-pandemic.[161]

McKinsey found that digital adoption "has grown strongly, even among the most 'digitally resistant' customers," and its article came to a similar conclusion:

"It's likely that many customers who have converted to digital services will stick to them after the immediate health crisis is over. Companies who make this shift to digital and deliver superior experiences have an opportunity to increase adoption and maintain these customer relationships after the crisis."[162]

Convenience

Although convenience has been a hallmark of customer experience forever, it became critically important during the pandemic. "Curbside pickup" became a hot trend for restaurants, grocery stores, and retailers. And it's not just pizza that can be delivered anymore. Companies as diverse as meal preparation boxes, pharmacies, pet supplies, alcohol, and even car dealerships got into the delivery game out of necessity because their customers were stuck at home.

According to Statista, the grocery delivery app Instacart saw month over month growth of more than 200 percent as the pandemic began.[163]

I remember waiting nearly two weeks for an appointment to get my bicycle repaired, but then the local shop picked it up from my garage and dropped it back off when it was ready. Good thing since my car isn't big enough to haul a bicycle, but I also wasn't ready to venture into the repair shop.

In customer experience, the opposite of convenience is friction, and friction can cause customers to quickly abandon your business for an easier journey.

"The more steps, complications, and time it takes to complete a purchase or connect with you, the more likely your customers will drop out of your sales funnel and jump to the competition," according to Podium, adding that to reduce friction, "transparent, accurate communication and convenience is key."[164]

Multiple ways to reduce friction in the customer journey include:

- Providing options for curbside pickup, in-store pickup, or delivery
- Engaging with customers on the channels of their choice
- Offering multiple options for payment, including contactless
- Finding opportunities to reduce clicks or taps with every digital interaction
- Eliminating hold times by offering callbacks
- Enhancing self-service options so customers can resolve their own issues

Eighty-six percent of consumers say they expect local businesses to offer more convenient communication and services since the COVID-19 outbreak, and 85 percent say the convenience of an experience is important in deciding whether they will return to a business again and again.[165]

Wilkinson-Brown of Sitel Group noted that time is a critical component of convenience.

"The impact of COVID-19 has underlined how valuable time is as a commodity in an always-on, always-connected world," he wrote. "The idea of saving or winning back time is now a central tenet of CX."[166]

Now that customers have gotten used to new convenience features, don't be surprised if their expectations for such conveniences continue well after the pandemic ends. For example, even though I personally like grocery shopping, I got used to saving an hour and a half every weekend by choosing curbside pickup instead. That is a convenience feature that is likely to stick around.

Look for opportunities in your business to make things quicker and more seamless for your customers; they will surely appreciate it.

Communicate, Communicate, Communicate

In times of crisis, it's hard to overcommunicate as long as what you are saying has some utility. Customers want information that directly affects them and their families, and all communications should be written from that perspective.

Instead, companies often write from their own perspective, talking about all of the things "we" are doing instead of focusing on how it benefits "you" the customer.

In 2018, when the European Union's General Data Protection Regulation (GDPR) went into effect, companies flooded email inboxes with privacy policy updates. Similarly, as the COVID-19 pandemic began, customers were inundated with urgent announcements about safety measures from every company that had ever obtained their email address.

Many companies chose to just "check the box," sending largely templated emails detailing cleaning processes and including links to the Centers for Disease Control and Prevention (CDC) and other government agencies.

It wasn't enough, as most consumers tuned out these incessant emails, just like they did with the mandated privacy policy changes a couple of years ago.

Brokerage firm Charles Schwab took a different approach, sharing resources to help its clients during this difficult time:

> *To Our Valued Clients:*
>
> *At Schwab, we have a deep and abiding belief in seeing the world "through clients' eyes." That simple, powerful idea helps us stay focused on what's most important: living up to the trust you place in us every day.*
>
> *With so much uncertainty in the financial markets and concerns about COVID-19, investing for the future may seem more complicated than ever. Please know that every one of us at Schwab is committed to helping you meet your long-term investing goals. I also want to remind you of the resources available to you . . .*

The email goes on to describe three investing resources and reassure clients of additional capacity to serve them, so "despite market turbulence and disruptions in daily life, we're confident in our ability to be here for you, whatever comes our way." It also sets customer expectations by acknowledging that phone wait times are longer than usual.

The entire email is calm, customer-focused, and helpful; compare that to all of the emails that refer to the same CDC website and mention the same cleaning and sanitation methods. Many companies just sent recycled emails so they could check one item off their crisis plan. Schwab gave its customers confidence and useful support when they most needed it.

Get Creative

With so much confusion about retailers closing, then reopening, then reclosing, it was difficult for the industry to stay top-of-mind with customers. Indeed, companies across industries were challenged with how to respond to COVID-19 from a business perspective. For some industries, like events and hospitality, revenues dropped to zero in a matter of days.

Some companies quickly pivoted, using their facilities to make new products or services that were in high demand.

For example:

- Distilleries began manufacturing alcohol-based hand sanitizer.
- Apparel companies ranging from giant retailers to mom-and-pop Etsy sellers began making face masks.
- Automotive companies began manufacturing ventilators for hospitals.
- Beverage companies ranging from beers to Capri Sun produced and gave away filtered water.
- Rideshare companies transported food and medicine when passenger demand dropped.
- Pet shelters shifted to virtual visits and online adoptions to meet a sharp increase in demand.
- Keynote speakers like me offered alternative programming such as virtual talks, coaching, and even a CX game show.

So what would customers want from Starbucks, besides, of course, their favorite beverage and the ability to return to that "third place" with friends?

The coffee giant sent an email to customers offering a unique resource that was perfectly applicable for the pandemic's stay-at-home world: downloadable virtual backgrounds featuring real Starbucks stores.

"No matter where you are, you can feel like you are at your favorite Starbucks anytime with a new collection of virtual backgrounds for your next video meeting," the email read.

The collection featured images of Starbucks stores from around the world, including one in Japan with a ceiling design made from more than 2,000 wooden sticks. There were even video backgrounds of Starbucks Cold Brew and Nitro beverages.

As a large number of workers settled in to working from home and participating in videoconferencing services every day, many wanted to show some personality by customizing a virtual background. While most services come with a few preloaded backgrounds, it became cool and fun to personalize the experience.

Starbucks saw that as an opportunity to participate in a different yet familiar way in its customers' lives.

The campaign was brilliant in its simplicity. It fit perfectly with the Starbucks brand and was fun without being intrusive or salesy. It successfully tapped into the emotions people were feeling, among them the desire to return to "normal." And it likely wasn't costly because Starbucks already owned all of the images.

What can your company do to connect with customers during a difficult time?

First, find something that resonates with your customers at an emotional level. The pandemic presented a unique opportunity to show empathy to customers because we knew exactly what they were going through—the same thing we were.

Next, make sure that the concept connects back to your brand. Schwab offering virtual backgrounds of its bank branches or Starbucks offering stock market advice probably wouldn't work. Find something that is quintessentially your brand.

Finally, have fun! Gather some of your most creative (and funny) employees and brainstorm ideas for capturing your customer's hearts—and wallets.

Going Forward

One thing that will remain constant long after the COVID-19 pandemic is that customer experience will still be the one true competitive advantage. But how we execute it, and in what channels, will change.

People will still long for human interaction, but they'll know they can achieve it in multiple ways. My mother and my seventh grader now know how to use Zoom, and neither did before. Businesses, schools, and places of worship now know how to function virtually. Telemedicine quickly gained traction.

The virtual world does not go away just because the virus does.

"Crisis situations, while disruptive in the short-term, are often valuable learning opportunities for many organizations," wrote Avtex. "Not only will a crisis shine light on the effectiveness or ineffectiveness of your disaster planning, unforeseen events can also offer a glimpse into potential improvements to your organization's overall operations."[167]

So what will change for businesses going forward? Behold, a few predictions:

- Telecommunications companies will have to beef up internet speeds and capacity for everyone.
- Digital security will improve drastically as more people access work from new places.
- The medical and dental professions will step up infection control procedures permanently.
- Home offices will be transformed with better cameras, lighting, microphones, and other equipment.
- Many companies will permanently relax work-from-home policies, and corporate positions at every level will be available for remote workers.
- Business continuity planning skills will be in high demand as companies seek not to repeat their mistakes of insufficient advanced planning.
- Some companies will even opt to sell their buildings or stop paying huge sums of rent every month for office space that isn't used and will use that money instead to invest back into the business.

The most important prediction, however, is that customer experience will continue to be the ultimate differentiator for businesses in every industry.

Customer expectations have never been higher, and the companies that focus on meeting or exceeding those expectations every day will ultimately win.

With so many choices today, why should a customer choose you? It won't be because of a fancy new logo or the latest social media marketing campaign. It also won't be because of a slight price difference or one new feature that the competition doesn't have.

People buy from companies that treat them well and give them experiences that are worth talking about.

The companies highlighted in this book have demonstrated that getting customers to share their positive experiences is more powerful than any marketing campaign. To be like them, simply create your own remarkable experiences.

So what are you waiting for? Go out there and be WISER than the competition!

ABOUT THE AUTHOR

Dan Gingiss is an international keynote speaker, customer experience coach, and the chief experience officer of The Experience Maker, LLC.

His twenty-year professional career consistently focused on delighting customers, spanning multiple disciplines including customer experience, marketing, social media, and customer service. He held leadership positions at three Fortune 300 companies: McDonald's, Discover, and Humana.

Dan is the author of *Winning at Social Customer Care: How Top Brands Create Engaging Experiences on Social Media*, a host of the *Experience This! Show* and *Focus on Customer Service* podcasts, and a regular contributor to *Forbes*.

He has been named to several notable industry lists, including:

- "Top 50 Customer Service Influencers of the Decade" by Nextiva
- "Top 50 Thought Leaders to Follow on Twitter" by ICMI
- "50 Social Media Marketing Influencers to Follow" by TopRank Marketing
- "Top 100 Digital Marketers" by both Brand24 and BuzzSumo
- "Top Customer Service Influencers" by Fit Small Business
- "15 Influencers Changing the CX Game" by WalkMe

Dan earned a BA in psychology and communications from the University of Pennsylvania and an MBA in marketing and operations from the Kellogg School of Management at Northwestern University. A native Chicagoan, he is a lifelong Chicago Cubs fan, a licensed bartender, and a pinball wizard.

For more information, please visit www.dangingiss.com.

ENDNOTES

1   Dan Gingiss, *Winning at Social Customer Care: How Top Brands Create Engaging Experiences on Social Media* (North Charleston, SC: CreateSpace Independent Publishing Platform, 2017), 15.

2   Internet Live Stats website.

3   Mike Ewing, "71% More Likely to Purchase Based on Social Media Referrals [Infographic]," June 28, 2019.

4   "Heuristics," *Psychology Today* website.

5   "Closing the CX Gap: Customer Experience Trends Report," Acquia, 2019.

6   "Sitel Group Report Reveals Brand Loyalty Is Only as Good as Your Last Customer Experience," Sitel Group, November 14, 2018.

7   "The Customer Experience Tipping Point," Medallia and Ipsos, 2019.

8   Ibid.

9   Ibid.

10 Stephanie Izard, Q&A Session at the Oracle Executive Roundtable at Izard's the Little Goat Diner in Chicago, May 20, 2019.

11 Gingiss, *Winning at Social Customer Care*, 4.

12 Tom Karinshak, Zoom interview, June 11, 2020.

13 "Deliver the CX They Expect: Customer Experience Trends Report," Acquia, 2019.

14 Ibid.

15 Ibid.

16 "Zendesk Customer Experience Trends Report 2020," Zendesk, 2020.

17 "5 Ways to Stay Ahead of the Competition," Podium, 2020.

18 John Coldwell, "How to Conduct Business to Business Customer Satisfaction Surveys," *CSM*.

19 "The Customer Experience ROI Study," Watermark Consulting, January 14, 2019.

20 Rachel Diebner et al., "Adapting customer experience in the time of coronavirus," McKinsey & Company, April 2020.

21 "The State of B2B Customer Experience Report," GetFeedback, 2020.

22 Ibid.

23 Ibid.

24 Lauren Fisher, *Customer Experience 2020,* eMarketer.

25 "The Best Brands and Industries for Customer Experience 2020," Brandwatch, 2020.

26 "Psychology of Choice," Psychologist World website.

27 Ibid.

28 PepsiCo, "Oh Hi! Meet bubly™ Sparkling Water and #CrackASmile," Cision PR Newswire, February 8, 2018.

29 Amelia Lucas, "PepsiCo earnings top estimates on strong snack and beverage sales, company backs 2019 forecast," CNBC website, July 9, 2019.

30 Fisher, *Customer Experience 2020,* eMarketer.

31 "The State of B2B Customer Experience," GetFeedback.

32 "Zendesk Customer Experience Trends Report 2020."

33 Domino's Pizza website—Carryout insurance.

34 Ibid.

35 Domino's Pizza website—Delivery insurance.

36 Imperfect Foods website—Our Mission.

37 Dan Gingiss, interview with Melissa Sprau, *Experience This!,* "Episode 92: Discover How Listening to Customers Can Help Even the Most-Maligned Industries Improve Their CX," podcast audio, March 10, 2020.

38 Dan Gingiss, interview with Allie Pleiter, *Experience This!,* "Episode 86: Discover How to Deliver a Truly Great Customer Experience," podcast audio, December 31, 2019.

39 "Benefits of Scent," FreshScents website.

40 Dan Gingiss, interview with Naftuly Kraus, *Experience This!*, "Episode 75: How to Live up to the Standard of Making a Customer's Entire Day," podcast audio, October 15, 2019.

41 Ellen Warren, "A stiff whiff can cut your raving craving," *Chicago Tribune*, October 19, 2011.

42 Kraus, *Experience This!*

43 Christopher Bergland, "How Does Scent Drive Human Behavior?," *Psychology Today*, June 29, 2015.

44 Alicia Phaneuf, "Here is a list of the largest banks in the United States by assets in 2020," *Business Insider*, August 26, 2019.

45 "Deliver the CX They Expect," Acquia.

46 Ibid.

47 Ibid.

48 "Do People Trust Charities? Study by BBB's Give.org Uncovers Pitfalls," Better Business Bureau website, May 5, 2020.

49 Dan Gingiss, "How Target Made Building Your Own Furniture into A Positive Experience," Forbes.com, November 16, 2018.

50 "5 Ways to Stay Ahead of the Competition," Podium.

51 Ramona Sukhraj, "7 must-have word-of-mouth marketing strategies [Infographic]," IMPACT website, April 7, 2018.

52 Lex Monson, Zoom interview, May 14, 2020. All quotes from Monson are from the same interview.

53 Fever-Tree website—Mediterranean Tonic Water.

54 Fever-Tree website—Indian Tonic Water.

55 "Starbucks Weaves Its Magic with New Color and Flavor Changing Unicorn Frappuccino," Starbucks Stories, April 18, 2017.

56 Ibid.

57 Evan Tarver, "Why the 'Share a Coke' Campaign Is So Successful," *Investopedia*, September 24, 2019.

58 Michelle Herbison, "'Share a Coke' campaign increased US sales for the first time in a decade," *Marketing* magazine (Australia) website, September 30, 2014.

59 Ben Rooney, "'Share a Coke' is back with more of your names on bottles," CNN Business website, August 14, 2015.

60 Sarah Homewood, "Coke takes 'Share a Coke' one step further," *Adnews* (Australia), May 13, 2015.

61 Tarver, "Why the 'Share a Coke' Campaign Is So Successful."

62 Dennis P. Carmody and Michael Lewis, "Brain Activation When Hearing One's Own and Others' Names," US National Library of Medicine, September 7, 2006.

63 "Musée d'Orsay," Wikipedia website.

64 Elizabeth Stamp, "Paris's Musée d'Orsay Hires Its First Instagram Artist-in-Residence," *Architectural Digest* website, January 10, 2020.

65 "Ally Banksgiving: When a Simple Call to Your Bank Turns into a Big Surprise," Ally Bank website, November 20, 2018.

66 Alex Cornell, "I'm On Hold," Track #6 on *2014 Acoustic*, 2014.

67 Jesse Cole, video conference interview, May 4, 2020. All quotes from this case study are from the same interview.

68 Christina Gough, "Teams of Major League Baseball ranked by revenue in 2019," Statista, April 29, 2020.

69 "Major League Baseball Miscellaneous Year-by-Year Averages and Totals," *Baseball Reference* website.

70 Gingiss, *Winning at Social Customer Care*.

71 "We awarded one customer $10,000 for doing what no one does, but always should," Squaremouth website.

72 Caitlin O'Kane, "Woman reads fine print on insurance policy, wins $10,000 in hidden contest," CBS News website, March 6, 2019.

73 "We awarded one customer $10,000 . . .," Squaremouth.

74 "Motorola Solutions—Moments that Matter," YouTube, October 2, 2013.

75 Chewy website—About Us.

76 Dan Gingiss, interview with Michael Bergman, *Experience This!*, "Episode 17: How Customer Experience Creates Word-of-Mouth Marketing," January 16, 2018.

77   Dan Gingiss, interview with Mariangel [No Last Name Given]," *Experience This!*, "Episode 17: How Customer Experience Creates Word-of-Mouth Marketing," January 16, 2018.

78   Dan Gingiss, interview with Mariangel [No Last Name Given]," *Experience This!*, "Episode 50: Always Make It about the Customer," November 27, 2018.

79   Dan Gingiss, video interview with Mary Drumond, *The Experience Maker Show,* "Episode 1—Mary Drumond," February 6, 2020.

80   *Experience This!*, Episode 50.

81   Ibid.

82   Zane Safrit, "Highlights from Talking with Chris Zane, Owner of Zane's Cycles," March 26, 2011.

83   Martin Wilkinson-Brown, "How Coronavirus Is Shaping Consumer Trends," Sitel Group, July 7, 2020.

84   "The Best Brands and Industries for Customer Experience 2020," Brandwatch.

85   Medallia and Ipsos, "The Customer Experience Tipping Point."

86   Ibid.

87   Dan Gingiss, interview with Madeline Piercy (née Aman), "Episode 33—How the Largest Utility in the U.S. Helps Customers Weather the Storm in Social Media," *Focus on Customer Service* podcast, June 6, 2017.

88   Slalom_build website, Hyatt case study.

89   Ibid.

90   "Consumers Have Humanlike Relationships with Brands," *Business News Daily*, February 13, 2020.

91   "The Best Brands and Industries for Customer Experience 2020," Brandwatch.

92   Ibid.

93   Fisher, *Customer Experience 2020,* eMarketer.

94   Ibid.

95   Ibid.

96   Matthew Dixon, Karen Freeman, and Nicholas Toman, "Stop Trying to Delight Your Customers," *Harvard Business Review,* July-August 2010 issue.

97   "Known error," Wikipedia website.

98   "Bounce rate," Google Analytics Support website.

99   "American Express and Discover Tie for Highest Rank in Customer Satis-faction," J.D. Power website, August 28, 2014.

100 "The State of B2B Customer Experience," GetFeedback.

101 Ibid.

102 Jim Tincher, "The Power of Moments: A Q&A with Chip and Dan Heath," Heart of the Customer website, December 13, 2017.

103 Tom Karinshak, Zoom interview, June 11, 2020.

104 Fisher, *Customer Experience 2020,* eMarketer.

105 Nilay Patel, "Everything is too complicated," *The Verge* website, January 7, 2018.

106 Ibid.

107 "Choice overload," Behavioral Economics website.

108 "Deliver the CX They Expect," Acquia.

109 "4 basic health insurance terms 96% of Americans don't understand," Policygenius, January 24, 2018.

110 APY takes into account both the interest rate and the ability of money to compound over time to give what is considered to be the more accurate idea of what money could earn in a year than the basic APR.

111 "58% Of Bank Content Inaccessible to the Average American: An Investi-gation into the Communication of 50 of The U.S.' Largest Banks," Visib-leThread, 2019.

112 "U.S. Health Insurers Struggle to Communicate with Their Audience," VisibleThread, 2018.

113 Ibid.

114 "58% of Bank Content . . .," VisibleThread.

115 "U.S. Health Insurers . . .," VisibleThread.

116 "58% of Bank Content . . .," VisibleThread.

117 Ibid.

118 Ibid.

119 Dan Gingiss, "New Research Shows Website Navigation May Be Losing You Customers," Forbes.com, September 27, 2018. Citation applies to all quotes from Basch.

120 ISO 9241-210:2019(en).

121 Jakob Nielsen, "How Long Do Users Stay on Web Pages?" Nielsen Norman Group, September 11, 2011.

122 "25 Great Quotes from Dale Carnegie That Make Us Want to Enjoy Our Life to the Full," Bright Side website.

123 "Deliver the CX They Expect," Acquia.

124 "Highlights from Talking with Chris Zane . . ." Safrit.

125 "Zendesk Customer Experience Trends Report 2020."

126 Ibid.

127 Ibid.

128 Medallia and Ipsos, "The Customer Experience Tipping Point."

129 Ibid.

130 "2017 Customer Service Barometer," American Express, 2017.

131 "Zendesk Customer Experience Trends Report 2020."

132 Ibid.

133 Dan Gingiss, interview with Lori Brown, *The Experience Maker Show,* "Episode 10—Lori Brown," April 9, 2020.

134 Ibid.

135 Katie Canales, "Some of San Francisco's robot-run restaurants are failing. It could simply be that we still want to be served by humans, not machines," *Business Insider*, January 12, 2020.

136 Ibid.

137 "What is a Chatbot?," Oracle website.

138 "Deliver the CX They Expect," Acquia.

139 Denise Lee Yohn, "Why Every Company Needs a Chief Experience Officer," *Harvard Business Review*, June 13, 2019.

140 "Zendesk Customer Experience Trends Report 2020."

141 Frédéric Durand, "The rise of the Chief Experience Officer," *CEO Monthly* website, August 31, 2018.

142 Ibid.

143 Dan Gingiss, "What Is a Chief Experience Officer and Why Does a Company Need One?," Forbes.com, December 17, 2019.

144 Ibid.

145 Tom Karinshak, Zoom interview, June 11, 2020.

146 Ibid.

147 Dan Gingiss, "How to Respond to Customers and Employees During a Pandemic," 2020.

148 Diebner et al., "Adapting customer experience in the time of coronavirus."

149 Ibid.

150 "5 Ways to Stay Ahead of the Competition," Podium.

151 Will Kenton, "Business Continuity Planning (BCP)," *Investopedia* website, July 24, 2020.

152 Dr. Mary McNaughton-Cassill, "We Could All Use Some Psychological First Aid," *Psychology Today*, July 16, 2020.

153 "5 Ways to Stay Ahead of the Competition," Podium.

154 Martin Wilkinson-Brown, "How Coronavirus Is Shaping Consumer Trends," Sitel Group, July 7, 2020.

155 Diebner et al., "Adapting customer experience in the time of coronavirus."

156 "5 Ways to Stay Ahead of the Competition," Podium.

157 Fabricio Dore et al., "Connecting with customers in times of crisis," McKinsey: April 2020.

158 "A Four-Phased Approach to Delivering Effective Customer Experience During a Crisis," Avtex, 2020.

159 Ibid.

160 Martin Wilkinson-Brown, "How Coronavirus Is Shaping Consumer Trends," Sitel Group.

161 Ibid.

162 Diebner et al., "Adapting customer experience in the time of coronavirus."

163 Jan Conway, "Increase in grocery delivery app downloads due to coronavirus outbreak U.S. 2020," Statista website, August 19, 2020.

164 "5 Ways to Stay Ahead of the Competition," Podium.

165 Ibid.

166 Martin Wilkinson-Brown, "How Coronavirus Is Shaping Consumer Trends," Sitel Group.

167 Avtex, "A Four-Phased Approach to Delivering Effective Customer Experience during a Crisis."

A free ebook edition is available with the purchase of this book.

To claim your free ebook edition:

1. Visit MorganJamesBOGO.com
2. Sign your name CLEARLY in the space
3. Complete the form and submit a photo of the entire copyright page
4. You or your friend can download the ebook to your preferred device

Print & Digital Together Forever.

Snap a photo   Free ebook   Read anywhere